Thomas Prescott

Christianity made science

A life's thoughts on religion and morals

Thomas Prescott

Christianity made science
A life's thoughts on religion and morals

ISBN/EAN: 9783337131883

Printed in Europe, USA, Canada, Australia, Japan

Cover: Foto ©Lupo / pixelio.de

More available books at **www.hansebooks.com**

CHRISTIANITY MADE SCIENCE;

OR,

A Life's Thoughts

ON

RELIGION AND MORALS.

BY THE

REV. THOMAS PRESCOTT, M.A.,

VICAR OF CADDINGTON.

WILLIAMS AND NORGATE,
14, HENRIETTA STREET, COVENT GARDEN, LONDON;
AND 20, SOUTH FREDERICK STREET, EDINBURGH.

1888.

[*All Rights reserved.*]

LONDON:
PRINTED BY C. GREEN AND SON.
178, STRAND.

To All whom

In Life's chequered Journey

I have ever known.

A PRELIMINARY WORD TO THE READER,

WHICH MAY POSSIBLY SAVE HIM THE TROUBLE OF GOING BEYOND THESE FEW INTRODUCTORY LINES.

WHO is the reader of these Thoughts? To whom in particular are they addressed? Let us try to define our reader. He is, in the first place and chiefly, a religious man. How, indeed, should one who is not religious care for religion, either in its scientific aspect or in any other respect? He is also a man of a scientific mind; otherwise, though he might care for religion, he would not care for science as well, consequently not for this treatise. He is, in fact, both scientific and religious, not merely one or the other. Many there are on the one hand religious, and not a few on the other hand scientific; but how many are there *both at once*, their religion sanctifying their science, and their science intellectualizing their religion?

The reader we have in our mind is, moreover, as to his feelings, a profoundly dissatisfied man; he is discontented, that is, in the highest degree with the state of religion as he finds it around him. He certainly cannot think of calling it science; he almost hesitates to call it religion. What is he to do? Is he to acquiesce and take rank simply with the many? No; he will not do that. He will try to ascertain for himself and independently what the truth is in religion; he will attempt to distinguish between the true and the false in his beliefs. He will find out a scientific method if he can. Nor will he do this thing, if it is to be done at all, by halves. He is a bold and honest man; he will follow the truth, whithersoever it goes. Even should the truth seem to be going exactly the way he would not have it go at any particular time, he will loyally follow it, nevertheless, having faith in it and being confident that it will in the end bring him to the "haven where he would be." He not only thinks, which is easy as men generally call thinking, but thinks his matter *out*, which is another thing quite.

Such, in their main features, are the characteristics of the man with special reference to whom these Thoughts are put on paper. Where is this well-equipped individual to be found? To such a one, wherever he is to be met with, we commend the following pages. They are for him, and for him alone; and we now, at the outset, endeavour to delineate him, mentally and religiously, in the main bearings of his character, in order that we may not put any one who does not more or less answer to the portraiture, to the disappointment of going beyond these premonitory words touching the personality of the reader.

Hast thou faith? Thou hast. Art thou dissatisfied with faith when it stands alone? Thou art. Dost thou wish for some confirmation of thy beliefs? If thou entertainest no such wish, put this book down almost before thou hast taken it up. It is not a book for thee; but if, on the contrary, thou dost insist upon some corroboration of thy Christian evidences, cast not this my endeavour aside, but bestow upon it thy best consideration. It is calculated to afford thee at all events peace of *mind* in the matter of thy religion. It aims at assigning to *the intellectual element a place, and its rightful place*, in religion. Its design is, in short, to secure a perfect obedience to that first and great commandment, "Thou shalt love the Lord thy God," not only "with all thy heart and with all thy soul," but "*with all thy mind*" (Matt. xxii. 37). The mind is the regulator and conservator of religion. Without the intellect, religion is a mere instinct. A religion of the heart alone is an imperfect thing; there needs to be added thereto a religion of the intellect if it is to be made perfect.

PREFACE,

IN WHICH IS SET FORTH THE SCOPE AND
ORIGIN OF THE THOUGHTS.

How came these Thoughts to be written? Or rather, how came they to be thought? for writing would seem to follow as a matter of course. Some hints as to their origin may not only be of interest in themselves, but they will perhaps best serve the purpose of an introduction, and more especially in two not unimportant respects. For one thing, a word or two in the way of explanation will stamp these apparently unconnected Thoughts with such a mark of unity and cohesion as they do not outwardly and visibly seem to possess; they appear, indeed, on the surface of them, not as a connected whole, but simply as isolated and disconnected units of truth—so far, indeed, as we may presume to call them truth, seeing they have not as yet undergone the ordeal of the independent and impartial judgment of other minds and not "been found wanting." And, again, some opening-out of the circumstances under which they were written will make clear that they embody an actual experience, that they are living thoughts, so to speak, and not an abstraction or imagination of difficulties that might be supposed to originate in the mind of the writer; but difficulties which actually did arise, every one of them, and which may be expected to be met with by others similarly constituted and in the like circumstances. A chapter out of the author's autobiography—not a literal extract, however, but the biography compressed and in a sense re-modelled—will substantially show how these Thoughts arose, what course they took, and what resting-place they finally found.

Doubts as to the truth and credibility of Christianity may be of two kinds. They may be merely personal, so as to affect the individual himself only; or they may be abstract, and so have the widest possible scope. The former kind of doubt concerns simply our own individual salvation, and embodies the question, Am I in the way of salvation myself? without any reference to the salvation of any other individual. The other sort of doubt is as wide as the whole range of religion, and challenges its very reality. Is there a redemption for man at all? Is Christianity itself true? If it is, I have no insuperable difficulty as to my own salvation, for I should assuredly use the means; if it is not, there ends the matter. With the former, or, as we may call them, the selfish category of doubts, we have nothing to do in these Thoughts, the writer never having been in the least troubled with them. It is with the latter sort of doubt only that we have any concern here, that which asks, and seems to ask in vain, the infinite and all-absorbing question, not, Is there a salvation for me? but, Is there a salvation for man at all?

We may remark by the way, that as regards doubts concerning our own salvation, as compared with doubts affecting the matter of salvation itself, the former are more charitably construed by the Christian world than the latter; indeed, that the former are in favour rather than otherwise, while the latter are thought to savour in their very nature of what is called infidelity. Let a man doubt as to his own religion as much as he will, and his character as a religious man by no means suffers; on the contrary, it is rather heightened thereby, his doubts being regarded as a sign of humility and self-distrust. But let him call in question in any way the truth and credibility of Christianity in the abstract, and his reputation as a man of religion is at once as good as gone; he is an infidel, and there an end. How is this?

That it is so, all will acknowledge; but whether it is rightly so, we shall probably be in a position to see more clearly at the end of these Thoughts than we do now at the beginning.

We are all of us free from doubts of all sorts to begin with. We are "little children;" and one main characteristic of little children is, not to doubt or cavil, but to take things for granted, and as they seem to be. Are minds ever so constituted as to be hermetically sealed against doubts, not only at first, but from first to last, from infancy to gray hairs? There may be minds so fortified or so empty as never to experience doubt; but whether or not, we are not concerned with their case. Besides, such individuals are not in themselves characters of interest. Either they do not care for religion in the earnest sense of the word, or, if they have minds at all, they have never turned their intelligence seriously to the solution of the great problems of religion. But be the experience of others what it may, doubts in the writer's case made themselves felt in what we may not improperly call the "fulness of time." The time for doubts came, and doubts came with the time. How did these questionings originate? What was the occasion?

When hardly arrived at manhood, a somewhat protracted illness took me. The visitation went hard with me. During my sickness, no religious thought troubled in any way my mind; and I may add that up to that period I had been for the most part indifferent as to matters of religion—not professedly so, much less to the extent of outward disregard of religion, but simply as to the mind, no religious thoughts having ever seriously engaged my attention. But now this indifference passed away, and, as it proved, for ever. There are many conversions in a man's life, and this was one of mine, from indifference to a deep concern as to future and eternal things. Recovery brought reflection, and I began to take myself to task. The result of this self-examination was found to be most unsatisfactory. What did I know practically, or even theoretically, of Christianity? Wherein lay my concern for it? What if my earthly career had been cut short when it seemed to be coming to a standstill? Was I not a nominal Christian, and nothing more? I resolved that I would not lie under the dark shadow of these self-accusations any longer; I would at least make myself an intelligent believer. So I resolved and so I acted. I gave myself up to serious reading and meditation, and to more than meditation. I would go to the fountain-head. In particular I entered upon a close study of St. Paul's Epistles, but not, I confess, to much practical purpose.

What was the result? Not at all what I expected. With thinking came, not clearness of mind and increase of faith, as I had hoped, but, on the contrary, darkness and perplexity of soul set in. The more I thought, the more I doubted. I looked round upon my religious neighbours for deliverance from this spiritual thraldom, but I found none. My thoughts now began to be fixed, not so much on my own state, as on the truth of Christianity itself. Was there really anything in religion? Time went on; but these doubts did not exhibit any symptoms of passing away or abating. On the contrary, they seemed to have taken up their quarters as if of right, as it were an invading host in an enemy's country. The more I had to do with them, even in the way of combating them, the more firmly did they seem to have me in their power.

What, then, was at this period my state of mind as a whole in relation to religion? Let us pause for a moment in order to make this inquiry, that we may rightly understand what my exact position at this time was. Was I an infidel? God forbid! Not an infidel, but that which in some ears sounds quite as ill-omened, a sceptic—a condition of mind which perhaps bears a worse character than it deserves. The difference between scepticism and unbelief is not of degree merely, but of kind. They are of different faculties of our complex and mysterious nature. Unbelief and scepticism are of "two houses." Unbelief is of the heart, and scepticism of the intellect. Heart and understanding do not of necessity concur in the matter of religion. The heart may believe, and the intellect may refuse to ratify this belief. It may interpose all manner of objections, and those not of necessity dishonest objections. Suppose the heart to give its voice in favour of religion, the intellect has the right of criticising and cross-examining, and seldom does it forego this right when it is an intellect worthy of the name.

A sceptic is not, we must always remember, necessarily an irreligious man; in fact, as a rule, we may say that he is not. He may be, and frequently is, quite the contrary. His misfortune is to be a man of thought. He is one not unfrequently whose mind has not yet been brought to admit what his heart and affections have willingly accepted. The language of the sceptic, were he to employ Scripture to express himself, would be, "Lord, I believe" (in my heart); "help thou mine" (intellectual) "unbelief." An infidel is a different stamp of man altogether: he is one who in his heart rejects the gospel; he has no liking for it, and his mind follows willingly the dictates of his affections. If you have to do with an infidel, do nothing; if you have to do with a sceptic, do not exhort him to go back to his old simplicity—that he cannot do—but to go on to the new and better experience which awaits him. So my state at this crisis of my Christian experience was religiously that of mind against heart, and heart against mind. Whether, if I had been left to wrestle with these sceptical thoughts single-handed, I should ever have come off conqueror, is not certain; perhaps I might have got the better of them eventually. But there is in this case no need of conjecture; a deliverer, as a matter of fact, appeared on the scene of these spiritual conflicts; that champion was no other than Bishop Butler. What did Bishop Butler do for me, and what did he fail to do?

The argument of Butler in his Analogy is well known. It professes to show—and shall we not admit does show?—the insufficiency and inconclusiveness of certain objections— to wit, those of a Deistical nature—against the truths of Christianity. How far may this overthrow of Deistical objections be held to prove that that against which they are vainly urged, viz. Christianity, is true? Or, to apply the principle as widely as possible, how far would the proved nothingness of *all* objections against Christianity prove Christianity to be true? Suppose the annihilation of all possible objections against the truth of Christianity to be an accomplished fact, to what would this demolition amount as a proof that the Christian revelation is true? Practically to little or nothing. It is at best negative testimony on behalf of Christianity. For example, though we should disprove effectually all the charges brought against some particular individual, this exculpation does not absolutely demonstrate that the man in question is all a man ought to be. The negative does not imply a positive. He is free from the faults imputed to him, but where are his virtues? Where is his perfection of virtue? The presumption is a very strong one, we admit, in the man's favour, that he is not merely negatively but positively good; but it is only a presumption. So Butler's argument, whatever be its value indirectly, is not of the nature of a proof-positive in affirmation of the truth of Christianity. He challenges you to prove that in certain particulars Christianity is false or impossible; but that is not the same thing precisely as proving it to be not only possible but true. He pleads, Not guilty, and his plea must be allowed. His proof, however, is a negative and indirect one; the proof-positive must be sought elsewhere.

Such is the value of Butler's argument when so extended as to meet objections universally against Christianity. But Butler, as we have said, does not profess to deal with objections universally against the truth of Christianity. His argument applies mainly to those which are of what we may call a Deistical character. He is arguing against men who acknowledge a God of Nature, but who deny a God of Revelation; and his *argumentum ad hominem* is as much as to say to them that they are bound to be more than Deists or less—that the objections which they find in a revelation which they do not admit, are already to be met with in those works of creation in which they experience no such difficulties. So Butler's argument is not only at best a negative one, but it may or may not meet your or my particular difficulties, whatever those difficulties may be.

Of what value, then, would Butler's argument be to me in my then state of mind, his reasonings being what I have attempted to reproduce, and supposing that I have represented Butler and his influence upon myself accurately? Of this accuracy, of course, it is impossible to be quite certain, inasmuch as impressions stamped upon the mind at a comparatively early stage of existence must undergo in course of time changes corresponding to those which the mind itself is liable to; so that what we take to be a simple recollection may be by no means so simple as we imagine, but a sort of mixed impression made up of *then* and *now*. Allowing, however, my present impressions to be substantially correct, Butler's work could not be expected to produce upon me any great or soul-stirring effect. For, in the first place, my individual objections were not those which the Bishop directly controverts; they were not of a Deistical nature, but of another character altogether: they were those of a believer in revelation—only there were difficulties in the way which seriously interfered with, if they did not effectually counteract, this belief. And, for another thing, whereas Butler undoubtedly furnished me, in his refutation of certain doubts of a particular character, with a presumption, and a strong one, of the truth of revelation altogether, this proof was not the kind of proof I could be satisfied with. What I required was, not merely negative, but positive evidence of the truth of those things which I had so long and anxiously questioned; and this positive evidence is not in Butler, nor are we justified in looking for it there.

So Butler's Analogy might be expected to produce upon me little or no practical effect. However, as a matter of fact, its effect was not what we might have anticipated, its operation being what may be described as supernatural rather than in accordance with the ordinary connection of cause and effect. It is not too much to say that it quite, for a time at least, put an end to all my troubles. It turned all my scepticism at one sweep out of doors, and made me once more a believer pure and simple. How was this? The explanation would seem to be, that Butler's argument found me, not cold and critical, but eager and receptive, and wrought in me an enthusiasm which overleaped strict calculation and carried all before it. Alps upon Alps of doubts, which, if considered judicially, would have been insurmountable, were now level as the plains of Dura. The overthrow of the particular difficulties which Butler combats had so much weight with me in my then state of feeling, as to imply practically the downfall of all objections whatsoever. It was impossible for me to stop short at a presumption merely, however strong, in favour of Christianity, or to arrest my steps anywhere short of an absolutely final goal. If Christianity be as good as true, I said to myself, what is that but to say that it is true? What is the use of making distinctions where there is no practical difference? So the impulse which Butler had imparted to me carried me far beyond the scope of the celebrated Analogy. The moral effect of the Bishop's reasonings was unlimited as compared with their literal significance, which would have been of comparatively small force if left to themselves. The spirit vastly outran the letter.

Where, then, were my doubts now? They are gone, quite gone, "leaving not a rack behind," and I hoped gone for ever. So I fondly imagined. Now, thought I to myself in exultation of spirit, I am my old self again, my old happy, undivided self. I am now once more in that state of self-satisfied belief which was my enviable lot in former days, when doubt with its self-tortures had not as yet disturbed my Christian repose. But I was reckoning without my former unwelcome guests. They were away, it was true, but only for a time and in a degree. Doubt had not, as I had supposed, taken leave of me for ever. Its absence proved but to be a recoil. I soon began to perceive, and gradually more and more to find, that Butler, notwithstanding the good service he had seemed to do me, and indeed had rendered me for a season, was only speculatively of value. My old doubts began to re-appear on the scene as though they had never been put to the rout. Not so boldly as formerly, or with so defiant a mien, did they re-assert themselves; for had they not been worsted once, and made to quit their ground; and might not what had occurred once, happen again? But certainly here they were, and not looking as though they were here merely as passing guests.

What was to be done? Was a greater than Butler to be waited for, to do over again, and effectually, the work which had already been wrought for me, and ineffectually, because only for a time? And what good to me if he did re-appear? Whatever power he might exercise, experience was beginning to teach me that such vicarious championship is at best but a temporary relief. "Who would be free, themselves must strike the blow," is a maxim true of other slaveries than those of the outward man. Yes; it was clear that I had only upon myself to reckon; and that for help, if it came at all, I must be indebted to myself alone. What, then, could I effect for myself more than I had done? Was I to argue these bewildering points over again and re-argue them? Was I so to wrestle with them and overcome them, as finally to work out for myself a redemption which Butler had achieved for me only for too short a time? No; that resolve promised nothing. The truth is, I was tired to death of these internal wrangles, and, moreover, thoroughly convinced of their practical inutility. Was it not to thinking, and indeed to over-thinking, that I was indebted for all my perplexities; and was it likely that thinking would turn round upon itself, and eat itself up, and so get me out of the mire as completely as it had got me in? Could I but have kept clear of thinking, I thought within myself, I should never have fallen into this slough of despond. Was I to go on for ever in this uncertain and self-contradictory way, oscillating perpetually between the *No* and the *Yes* of the truth of Christianity, and never able to say either Yes or No finally and for ever? Was I always to be the sport of argument, or logic, or of the last speaker, whoever he might be, for or against the truth of revelation? Would it not be preferable, I was almost tempted to say, to know once for all that what I believe in is false, than thus never to be assured that it is one thing or the other? Better, would it not be, to end the conflict once for all somehow, than thus wear out my life to no purpose?

Thus did I ponder over these things; and, as I dwelt upon them, the suspicion at length began to force itself upon me and gradually to occupy my mind, till at last it had full possession of me, that possibly I was on the wrong system altogether, and that I was employing *some insufficient or unpractical method* of solving the great problem of Christianity, if indeed there was any method at all possible. Was I not laying the entire stress of religion philosophically upon mere thinking, and what was it but thinking that had created all my difficulty hitherto? True it was that thinking or speculation, in the form of Butler's Analogy, had given rest and delight to my weary soul; but that was only for a time, and the good deed speedily undid itself again. Where was I now? Hardly less wofully in the "horrible pit and miry clay" than before, notwithstanding Butler and his really welcome championship for a season. Where was I indeed but left to the tender mercies of my own thoughts, which I found to be prolific enough in creating difficulties, but powerless to silence or chase them away? The tribunal to which I have submitted my case persistently so far is, I reflected, that of thought or speculation, or call it what you will. Is this the court made and provided for such cases in the realm of reason or common-sense? At any rate, it is a most vacillating judgment-seat, at one time pronouncing Christianity to be true, at another time judging it to be false, and never giving any two consecutive judgments alike. No; speculation is not the legitimate tribunal, whatever else may or may not be. Religion is not speculation; it is a practical thing, the most purely and simply practical thing with which man has to do. Well, is there no practical court before which my case may be tried, so as to bring it to some intelligible and common-sense issue?

What is religion? The simplest thing in the world, would man only not confound that which God has made plain. What is it but this—that you are to walk in a certain prescribed way, and you will arrive at a certain promised end; that prescribed way being the way of faith and God's revelation, and this promised end being the fulfilment of the Bible's "many great and precious promises," a fulfilment which, be it observed, we are authorized to look forward to, not merely in the world to come, but in a measure in this present life? What is there of speculation here? What is there to puzzle or mystify the mind? All is practical, all is plain. What is the conclusion of the whole matter but "Fear God and keep His commandments"? Faith and obedience are practical virtues. Speculation may confuse them and bewilder us, but it is powerless to promote them. And what is experience, to crown all, but the absolute and irrefragable test of the right or wrong of the life we have preferred to lead? Do God's promises come true or not? Are they *Yea* and *Amen*, as they are affirmed to be, to the believer, or not? If they do come true, then Christianity is true. If they do not come true, then where is Christianity? The whole argument lies, intellectually, in an infinitely small compass.

The question then is, What shall I *do* if I would know whether Christianity is true? not, What shall I *think?* And the answer is plain: I will walk in the Christian way, and that not as a mere matter of form, but heartily and honestly. God being my helper, I will "run with patience the race that is set before me;" and then shall I know, and only then can I know, how much or how little reality there is in my creed. The truth of Christianity is life's problem; and what can I do better than employ my life in the elucidation of that mystery, which, whether as regards time or eternity, is alone worthy of my regard?

The more I considered this method, and the more I contemplated it on all sides, the more was I convinced of its intrinsic merits as the only true method, till at last it had full possession of me, and with my complete sanction. And why not be content, seeing that this method is not merely the only assured way of Christian evidence, but the path of true religion as well? It might indeed prove Christianity to be false—but what of that? It would at least prove something, and that something would satisfy at all events *my mind*, and I had no fear deep down in my heart as to satisfaction in any other sense.

But where are all my speculations now? They are vanished. No sooner did the truth break upon me that *religion is a practical thing* (as Butler himself somewhere confesses), and in no substantial sense speculative, than all my whilom doubts fled away as the darkness of night before the rising sun. Why, indeed, should they not take their flight, and for ever? Why should they ever again disturb my peace of mind? Would they even make the attempt? Had I not found a method, according to which I could conclude positively as to the truth or otherwise of religion if I would only be at the pains? What can speculation add thereto or take therefrom, with its empty parade of logic? Speculation is clearly nowhere. The reason, indeed, why I had dwelt so long under the dark and deadly shadow of doubt was, that I had ignorantly surrendered myself to a wrong method; though in mitigation of my thus wandering so far from the right path, I may be allowed to plead that it seems to be the method of no inconsiderable section of the Christian world. Now that I had found the true method (the only method), I was no longer tossed upon an infinite sea of doubt; "the peace of God keeps" at least "the mind."

The result is, that heart and mind, which parted asunder when these doubts first made themselves felt, are now at one again. But are they one again in the sense in which they were one ere I, this sentient, thinking being, could be said to have had, properly speaking, a Christian experience at all—that is, before doubts first fastened upon the mind? Not so; the two states, that of innocence and that of experience, are widely apart in character no less than in time. Outwardly, indeed, and objectively, this oneness of heart and mind is now precisely what it was in that, as I may term it, pre-sceptical period; but there is inwardly an immense difference between then and now, a difference worth all the toil and all the tribulation of the intervening stages. What is the religion of a little child? What is the religion of a father in Christ, of a veteran soldier of the Cross? What is the difference between the two? The religion of the former is indeed as yet an unsullied faith; but it is at the mercy of the first challenger, or it may be of the first suggestion of evil;

the latter is a broken faith which has been re-set, the characteristic of which restoration is, that no power on earth or from below can ever break it again. There is all the difference in the world between that condition of Christian innocence in which religion is first cradled, and that final stage of Christian experience which is on the way in due time to exclaim, "I have fought the good fight; I have finished my course; I have kept the faith."

Here ends the autobiography, so far as it has reference to, or throws light upon, the following Thoughts. It explains how the Thoughts came to be written, and shows that they are not a chaos or an abstraction, but a unity and an actual experience. In fact, the Thoughts are such as presented themselves as it were spontaneously to the writer for solution in the course of his meditations on the possibility of a Christian Science. They are put before the reader first of all under their respective headings, in a *Conspectus or Table of Thoughts*, and then an attempt is made to work them out severally in the order in which the Table presents them. And what is this order? In one sense it is no order at all: the Thoughts might just as well—not a few of them—have occupied some other place, so far as the general argument is concerned. Nevertheless, some consecutive order has been attempted, and, it is hoped, not altogether without success. The great point, however, is, as to whether these several Thoughts do or do not in their respective degrees conduce to the solution of the one great problem in hand, i.e. Christianity made Science. If they do serve this purpose, it is of small consequence in what relation they stand each one to the thought which immediately precedes or to the one which next follows. Truths are independent and in a sense isolated; they do not necessarily follow in a sequence. The word "therefore" does not invariably usher in a truth, nor the absence of it betoken some hollow or empty thing. Truths are seen, not concluded.

One word more to wind up the Preface. How comes it to pass, it may be asked, that morals occupy so large a place in these Thoughts, or indeed any place at all, seeing that the problem before us is a purely religious one? Why have we not kept to religion? The answer is that we have kept to religion, and that, in order to do so, it was necessary to take full account of morals and of their relation to religion. Religion without morals, notwithstanding all its grandeur, is a lame and impotent thing. Morals and religion are so interwoven that they cannot be kept apart, do what we will, either practically or scientifically considered. In discoursing on religion, you must take morals fully into account, or your religion is nothing—or worse!

CONSPECTUS,

OR

TABLE OF THOUGHTS.

	PAGE
I.—Faith the faculty of the Spirit and the source or origin of our primary religious perceptions	1
II.—On Faith as a faculty in its relation to Common Sense	6
III.—Faith and Scepticism, how related	10
IV.—Faith the preliminary stage of all Knowledge	14
V.—Religion and Science not antagonistic	21
VI.—Reason and Faith compared and contrasted	23
VII.—No need for more than Faith to begin with	25
VIII.—The sphere of Faith	26
IX.—Faith or Unbelief in itself proves nothing	28
X.—Faith up to a certain point good; beyond that point, evil	31
XI.—Faith must go on or go off; it cannot stand still	32
XII.—Galileo a pattern to the Believer as touching his Faith	37
XIII.—Man not indebted to Philosophy for the elements of Religion	39
XIV.—Suppose Philosophy could give us demonstration to begin with—what then?	41

		PAGE
XV.—Thanks to Philosophy for its endeavours, nevertheless		43
XVI.—Why are our religious ideas so indistinct? Different classes or orders of ideas		45
XVII.—Was a Revelation to Man necessary?		50
XVIII.—We may at least imagine a Revelation not necessary		51
XIX.—But fact does not confirm our imaginings		55
XX.—Why this discrepancy between imagination and fact?		59
XXI.—Man not left to himself as regards religious light		63
XXII.—But has God given us as much as possible?		64
XXIII.—To have given more would have been hurtful, not helpful		65
XXIV.—Wanted a Method by which Religion may be tried		72
XXV.—A scientific Method possible		74
XXVI.—Experience the test of Truth in Religion		77
XXVII.—Faith and Experience the two pillars on which Christianity rests		79
XXVIII.—The three stages of Religion: 1. Faith; 2. Works; 3. Experience		80
XXIX.—Christian Science not in itself Religion		85
XXX.—Experience no new test of Truth in Religion		89
XXXI.—Why has so simple a Method not been universally followed?		94
XXXII.—But is there no Method actually at work now?		101
XXXIII.—Difference between theological and scientific Method		103
XXXIV.—Descartes not with us in our Method		105

		PAGE
XXXV.—What a Science of Religion is not. M. Emile Burnouf		107
XXXVI.—Orthodoxy and these Thoughts		112
XXXVII.—Speculation no way to Christian Truth. Four reasons		115
XXXVIII.—Bishop Butler as to the worth of Speculation in Religion		119
XXXIX.—Human knowledge relative, not absolute		122
XL.—The Bible: its proper place in the Christian Scheme		123
XLI.—The Bible rests upon Christian Experience, not vice versâ		127
XLII.—The right way of dealing with Holy Scripture		129
XLIII.—Religion does not rest upon Bible or Church as a foundation		130
XLIV.—The Bible itself countenances a sign in confirmation of its Word		132
XLV.—Truth of Bible a conclusion, not a premiss		136
XLVI.—Morality and Religion, how related		139
XLVII.—Morality: its end and its aim		143
XLVIII.—Man has moral senses or faculties to begin with		144
XLIX.—Religion and Morals distinct, though connected		146
L.—Morality incomplete in itself as a practical goodness		147
LI.—Religion the complement of Morals and the fulfiller of the Law		151
LII.—Religion a usurper in general, particularly in the sphere of Morals		158
LIII.—Importance of determining whether of the two is greater, Morality or Religion		159

LIV.—Moral sense and Experience the two arbiters of Morals 162
LV.—Judaism and Christianity—in what relation do they stand to each other? 166
LVI.—Judaism and Christianity in matter one, in form diverse 173
LVII.—Is God angry with us when we are what is called critical in Religion? 177
LVIII.—Religion as to these Thoughts an individual concern only 179
LIX.—Notwithstanding any Knowledge we may acquire, we walk not by Sight, but by Faith, unto the end 187
LX.—Our Knowledge incommunicable as Knowledge 188
LXI.—Is it possible to draw the line between the Christian in his individuality and in his relation to Christendom at large? 191
LXII.—By what right have we taken in hand these Thoughts? 197
LXIII.—A forecast, or Christian Science in the future 213
LXIV.—Conclusion, wherein the writer bids adieu to the reader and leaves him his work to do 232

CHRISTIANITY MADE SCIENCE.

1.—FAITH THE FACULTY OF THE SPIRIT AND THE SOURCE OR ORIGIN OF OUR PRIMARY RELIGIOUS PERCEPTIONS.

RELIGION (*id quod religat*) is the connecting link between man and God, between man and the invisible world. Religion, when stated in its simplest terms, may be said to be a belief in God and in things eternal. This belief is the expression of the believing faculty in man, and an evidence of the actual existence of such a faculty. The object proves the eye, no less than the eye the object. That these beliefs do exist in us, and that not sluggishly and passively, but actively and vigorously, is simple matter of experience. Whence, then, are these beliefs, or how can they be accounted for, unless man, as he has bodily eyes for material objects, and eyes of the mind for things intellectual, has also an organ of the spirit for "things that are spiritually discerned"?

Say that a spiritual world really exists, how is man to be cognizant of that spiritual world, or hold converse with it, unless there be between the two worlds some channel of communication, and in man a power of spiritual apprehension? Things seen argue a seeing faculty. The unquestioned fact that there are in man—in man universally, we may say—beliefs, implies unquestionably the existence of a believing organ. This faculty also, it is certain, is distinct from any other of man's faculties, notably his intellect, the one with which it might seem to have most in common. Were faith a species of intellect, we should expect it to be strong in a man in proportion as his intellect is so. But we by no means find this to be the case, but rather the contrary; a plain proof that our religious faculty, whatever it may be, is not identical with the understanding, but that it is an independent sense, and serves other purposes than those of intellect—to wit, that it is the apprehension of those things that are spiritually discerned.

How, moreover, are we to account for inspiration and revelation as commonly understood, but on the assumption of a spiritual faculty in man to begin with? Revelation and inspiration are, in their common acceptance, intelligible solely on the presupposition of such a faculty. If inspiration and revelation are realities, it follows—or perhaps we ought to say, having regard to the order of time, it precedes—that the spiritual sense we attribute to man is a reality also. On the supposition of an organ in man whose province it is to take cognizance of things divine, we at once understand what is meant by inspiration in man. Inspiration is the greater illumination, the intensification of this power. An inspired man is a believer in a larger sense of the word faith than are believers generally—not, however, of course, so far as to transcend the limits between faith and sight. The believing faculties are raised for the time being to a higher power.

And, indeed, it seems but natural, and strictly in accordance with analogy, that if man is really endued by nature with distinctively religious faculties, these faculties should, in the privileged few and for particular purposes, rise so high as to become extraordinarily what we call inspiration. As there are men of what we style genius in natural things, in learning, science, art, why not also in the things of the kingdom of heaven, though we do not call this excellency of gift in this case by the name of genius? Faith, in short, as a faculty capable, as are all our faculties, of increase and diminution, accounts for inspiration; but what is to account for it if faith is not a faculty to begin with?

So also as regards revelation. What can revelation possibly mean except on the ground of an already existing faculty such as we take faith to be? Revelation is objectively what inspiration is subjectively. They amount to the same thing virtually. Revelation is literally the unveiling of that which is within the veil. But an object to be seen implies an eye to see with. If man has indeed a spiritual eye, we at once understand how a revelation can be made to him. On this supposition all is plain. But how if the eye is wanting or never existed? How if the man is "blind and cannot see afar off" or even near at hand? To what in man's spiritually dark nature is the revelation then to be made?

We find just the same difficulty in comprehending what is meant by revelation as we experienced in the matter of inspiration, and for the same reason. Revelation, equally with inspiration, implies a power of spiritual perception in man, and on this hypothesis alone can you attach any real and substantial meaning to the words inspiration and revelation ; they are words, and nothing more. Unless man has an eye of the spirit, no less than and distinct from any other eye that is in him, we cannot understand how he should ever have had any ideas at all outside the material limits of this world, even supposing the reality of such a world ; and certainly not how a faculty, of which he is not possessed to begin with, should ever be raised to the higher power of inspiration, or to an apprehension of the more special objects of revelation.

II.—ON FAITH AS A FACULTY IN ITS RELATION TO COMMON SENSE.

Faith, if we have rightly taken it to be a sense, man's spiritual sense, must be subject, as are the senses in general, to the laws and authority of common sense. Common sense is the common ground on which all the senses meet. "Il faut concevoir" (says Descartes, *Règles pour la direction de l'esprit*) "que tandis que le sens externe est mis en mouvement par l'objet, la figure qu'il reçoit est transportée vers une autre partie du corps appelée *le sens commun*." Common sense is the universal sense, that sense which takes cognizance of all the senses. Or we may say it is a compound of all the senses, however many there be, and in whatever proportions. Where the senses are few or feeble, common sense is of little value; on the other hand, however potent and multifarious the several senses may be, if there is no common sense, the individual so endowed is a mere creature of impulse, acting in accordance with those particular inclinations which may have possession of him for the time.

Man has many orders of senses or instincts —senses of the body, senses of the mind, a moral sense, a religious sense (which we call faith), a sense of shame, a sense of beauty; and we know not how many more might be catalogued, could we but map out human nature adequately. It is a matter of course, therefore, that there be some common ground on which all these senses may meet for the purposes of comparison and conclusion. Without a common sense as a sort of clearing-house, judgment or reasoning would be impossible; man would be at the mercy and under the dictation of his instincts alone. By means of the sense of hearing or sight, we hear or see; but common sense compares together, and draws a joint conclusion from, what we hear and see. Our bodily senses take cognizance of things tangible and visible; our thinking powers, of things intellectual; our religious sense or the sense of faith apprehends things invisible; and by virtue of common sense we bring together and draw conclusions from these several data of the individual senses.

Common sense is not, strictly speaking,

reason or judgment, but it furnishes the materials and ground-work necessary to our reason and judgment; nay, it is judgment, in so far as correct and wide general instincts may be termed judgments. A man of common sense is one who is well endowed with senses, and with the common basis on which all the senses meet. A man of genius is one in whom some special sense of an extraordinary character is unusually predominant. It is a most rare thing to find a man who is at once distinguished for genius and for common sense. A second Shakspeare is possible, but in the highest degree improbable. Men of genius are generally taken to be deficient in common sense; but the truth may be that some one sense so overpowers the senses as a whole that they suffer in comparison, or, it may be, are actually oppressed.

In particular, the relation in which faith as an individual sense stands to common sense as the aggregate and arbiter of all the senses, seems to be simply this. It is the province of faith as a faculty to say what is and what is not religion—to define religion, in short. But where the question is mixed, as most of our deliberations are—moral, religious, and social (or even more mixed still)—all in one, then it is not for faith or any single voice to determine the point at issue, but it must be referred for decision to the high court of the senses, the tribunal of common sense.

III.—FAITH AND SCEPTICISM, HOW RELATED.

Faith and scepticism in religion do not stand to each other in the relation of affirmative and negative of the same faculty. They are of different faculties. Faith is of the heart, or, may we say? of the will; scepticism is of the intellect or thinking powers. Faith is the eye of the spirit, the believing faculty, an inlet of the simple ideas of religion. It has for its objects, primarily, things invisible and eternal; and, secondarily, Christian revelation wherever contained, and especially in Old Testament and New Testament. This eye may be strong or weak, or it may be altogether blind, but it never can be more than blind. It may see nothing, but it never can affirm that there is nothing to be seen. Scepticism, on the other hand, is of a different nature and operation altogether. It is the result of the exercise of the intellect upon the primary and fundamental truths of religion, that is to say, the being of a God and the reality of an unseen world, or upon the facts of revealed religion.

Consequently, one and the same individual may be both a believer and a sceptic; a believer by virtue of that faith which is "the evidence of things not seen" (Heb. xi. 1), and a sceptic by reason of the exercise of his thinking powers (and as a result of that exercise) upon things invisible, which the sceptic tries to reason out, but in vain, seeing they are beyond reason, or rather antecedent to reason, being simple perceptions. Whether faith or scepticism shall in the end prevail, depends upon the relative strength of the intellectual and believing powers. Scepticism results from the impossible attempt to arrive at certainty in religion by means of speculation. There is no such way to certainty. The only path is that which every good man consciously or unconsciously treads—that of practice, not of speculation; that of doing, not of mere thinking. It is experience that must finally determine the all-important question of the truth of religion, not observation alone, however accurate and extensive.

Faith and experience are the two pillars on which religion philosophically and practically rests; faith for ideas and for facts whether primary or secondary, and experience to put these ideas to the test. And the only way that experience can take is that of a godly life according to the dictates of faith. "Fear God and keep His commandments" is the last word of the sceptical preacher, as it is the first word of all practical inquiries into the truths of religion. When any one prides himself upon his orthodoxy and upon his never having been troubled with doubts upon the subject of religion, what is this orthodoxy but as much as to say that he is not a thinking being, or at least not in matters of religion? Mere thinking must generate scepticism. Reasoning may be expected finally to vanquish scepticism, where the scepticism is of home origin and growth, and not an importation from elsewhere; but thinking must in the first instance beget this enemy and beclouder of faith.

Do not be afraid of honest doubts. Never shrink from the freest possible thought in religion; only beware of other people's doubts and insinuations. Beware also of foregone conclusions. Do not regard them as conclusions until they really are so. Your own sincere questionings can do you no harm; the scepticism of other people may.

You may not be able successfully to cope with the more formidable doubts of stronger or more subtle minds. Think for yourself; think boldly, and think to the end. "Unto the upright there ariseth a light in the darkness." You are sure, finally, if you are honest and courageous, and not afraid of looking truth in the face, to make your way through the darkness to the light beyond, where is no darkness at all.

IV.—FAITH THE PRELIMINARY STAGE OF ALL KNOWLEDGE.

That religion should begin in faith ought not to surprise us. It is a principle not peculiar to religion. Which of the exact sciences is there that was not of faith to begin with, be the belief true or false? What was the Ptolemaic system of astronomy but simple faith? The sun in that system is, according to the science of Shakspeare's day, merely a planet, albeit "the glorious planet Sol," and the earth is fixed and immovable, being no other than "this centre." Whence did the simple-minded philosophers of that unscientific period get all this? They had not proved their theory; they had not put it to any test; they did not care to do so; they simply believed. When proof comes in the person of Galileo, all this faith vanishes. So when we say that religion intellectually does, to begin with, lie within the domain of faith exclusively, we are only stating of religion now what was erewhile the position of even the exact sciences. Man never jumps into knowledge all at once. He does, however, rise gradually to knowledge. So it has been in astronomy and geology and other sciences.

We are not therefore to feel surprised that the same principle should hold in religion, and that, moreover, a longing should be felt and a genuine attempt made, on the part of those to whom religion is nothing if not truth, to put religion on a scientific foundation, on a basis of knowledge if possible, and no longer simply of faith. If we were not content with appearances in the case of the earth—if "I believe that the earth stands still" did not then permanently satisfy our minds—how could it be expected that we should regard mere appearances as fully and finally satisfactory now in the matter of heavenly things, and should be content to go on saying for ever, without any wish to go further, "I believe in God and in a world to come"?

Why should Christianity remain perpetually at the low point of dogma, the lowest of all stages on the road to truth, and not rather strive to rise to the rank of positive knowledge? Is astronomy or chemistry or geology to enjoy in this respect a glory which is denied to that spiritual kingdom which, so far as the material with which it has to deal is concerned, incomparably transcends all merely human heights of investigation? If religion is to stay for ever at this stage of intellectual development, what value can it be expected to have in the eyes of the man whose mind is cast in the scientific mould, even though the man of religion, who cannot have too much faith, may on this very account prize it all the more? Are religion and intellect to be in a state of perpetual divorce? Is religion to be cast on one side as an impracticable thing? Is the objector to be for ever asking, "Where are thy proofs, O Religion! not thy beliefs merely, but thy certainties," and no precise answer be returned?

But it may be you are afraid to go beyond faith, afraid to bring religion to some scientific test, even though you should have it in your power to do so. Perhaps you have no confidence in your faith, not fully believing that it is really worthy of the allegiance you pay to it, or that it is ready to answer all reasonable demands made upon it in the matter of its credentials. Be not a traitor to thy faith! Thou art a traitor if thou wilfully eschewest the scientific method, that is to say the only method, of arriving at truth. Do not, while professing to love thy religion above all things, show that thou hast no confidence in it whatever. Cast thy faint-hearted cowardice to the winds, or rather sink it in that bottomless abyss whence all such half-heartedness proceeds. Do with religion what is being done, and will be done more and more, in every field of human inquiry, until the rule is universal.

Put thy Christian beliefs to the test, and what will happen? Do not suppose that thy beliefs will all of them stand the fiery ordeal. Some of thy cherished opinions— we know not how many—will be found of no worth, "the baseless fabric of a vision;" but, on the other hand, things thou dost not now so much as imagine will be found gloriously certain, if it be indeed true, as thou believest, that "eye hath not seen, nor ear heard, neither have entered into the heart of man, the things which God hath prepared for them that love Him" (1 Cor. ii. 9).

Thou wilt have difficulties, we confess, in acting in this straightforward, decisive manner, difficulties not only from without, but from within. Thy prejudices are in the way. Dost thou say thou hast no prejudices? When didst thou cast them off? Thou hadst them once—thou must have had. All the impressions of thy mind stamped upon thee in thy infancy and early childhood, and before thou wast able to be on thy guard against false or imperfect judgments, were but so many prejudices and prepossessions. Whether true or false in themselves, they were, so far as thou wast concerned, literally *prejudicia*, that is, conclusions formed irrespectively of any prior judgment on thy part. When didst thou cast them off as unproven, if not as filthy rags? When didst thou test them in the crucible of reason, to try them whether they be the pure gold of the sanctuary? At what point of thy life and under what circumstances didst thou make the resolve to look truth full in the face, however much it might be against thee, and so open thy mind to the pure and simple perception of the white rays of truth?

The process of this casting off of old things and putting on of new is not easy; it is, moreover, so utterly repugnant to flesh and blood, that it is not likely ever to have left thy recollection. It is no less than tearing self from self, the self of the flesh from the self of the spirit. If thou hast never experienced and excruciatingly felt this rending asunder and consequent nakedness of spirit, so as to retain it still vividly in thy remembrance, thou art a man of prejudice, say what thou wilt; thou seest things not as they are in themselves, but as they are in thyself and through the medium of some more or less distorted or impure light, and thy prepossessed and precharged mind taints or warps all thy judgments.

V.—RELIGION AND SCIENCE NOT ANTAGONISTIC.

It is a common notion that Religion and Science are somehow in opposition, and that as one goes up the other goes down. The two are of different natures certainly, but there is no antagonism between them, if each is allowed to have its own place; indeed, they are the two things which most of all stand in need of each other's friendly countenance and support. Religion is the material to be dealt with, and science is the method of dealing intellectually with this divine material; and it is no argument against its right so to do, or against the obligation of religion to submit to the ordeal, that science has authority as regards also materials which are earthly and not divine; for the scientific method is one and universal. An earthly method, and divine materials for this earthly method to deal with, where is the contradiction, unless you are prepared to say that man himself, who is human, is incompetent to apprehend and appreciate what is divine?

There is only one method of arriving at truth, whatever be the material with which we have to do. Your ounce-weight is good for your ounce of gold no less than for your ounce of lead. A yard measure has just told off a quarter of a yard of calico: is it thereby degraded so as to be disqualified from taking the measure of a bale of silk? A divine method for things divine may sound well; but we are human and not divine, and, as human beings, must be content with a human method, whatever may be the nature of the material, terrestrial or celestial, with which we are concerning ourselves. A divine method, wherever it has been invented and applied—for it is man's invention — has unfortunately never been found to answer to its high-sounding title. Supernatural it may not inappropriately be termed, but only in the sense of "workmen who strive to do better than well," with the inevitable result of doing worse than well. Whatsoever is not according to nature even in religion, is false.

VI.—REASON AND FAITH COMPARED AND CONTRASTED.

Never ask, as some do, whether reason or faith is greater. The question arises from inconsiderateness, or at least forgetfulness, of how different reason and faith are in their nature and office, and how incapable they are of comparison. Faith is a witness as to fact; reason sits in judgment on the evidence which faith gives. To inquire whether is greater, is like asking in a court of justice whether the judge on the bench or the witness in the box is greater; or whether a piece of silk or the yard measure which tells it off occupies the higher position. Each has its own place, which the other is incompetent to fill. In one sense, that is as to intrinsic value, the piece of silk is greater; but in another sense, that of sitting in the seat of judgment, the yard measure is greater: it is, in fact, supreme if it be a true measure. Reason in religion is nothing, absolutely nothing, without faith, just as the occupation of a yard measure is gone where there is no material to be measured; but where there is such material, it is for reason, and for reason alone, to tell the length and breadth of it, and to say whether it be full measure or "weighed in the balances and found wanting."

Those who do only what they like in matters of religion (and their "name is legion, for they are many") will, as we may expect, demur to this supremacy assigned to reason, which, however, nature and the Bible have alike agreed to give it, and not we. Men of self-will naturally prefer to have the power of pronouncing for themselves what is to be the weight and measure of their religion; and, above all things, they would rather not refer the case to the standard weights and measures of the court of

Reason. Their reluctance is quite natural. Do not thou follow their example, or attempt to set things of faith and things of reason the one against the other. Things of faith are also things of reason. All things, without exception, are things of reason to the man of reason; to the man of unreason, nothing is.

VII.—NO NEED FOR MORE THAN FAITH TO BEGIN WITH.

Properly speaking, there could not be certainty in the evidences of Christianity to begin with, otherwise religion could not be of faith. The rich man in the parable demands evidences which are not of faith, but of sight, for his five brethren, and they are refused him. Nor need there, in the strict sense of the word, be positive evidence on behalf of Christianity to begin with, seeing that there is complete evidence on the other side to the effect that, to live according to this world, the only other possible life to lead is "vanity of vanities." We see at least that the world is false and worthless—there is no doubt on that score: what need we, therefore, practically to see without doubt that religion is true *to begin with?* There is, properly speaking, no competitor.

VIII.—THE SPHERE OF FAITH.

Keep religion within its own assigned domain as regards the universal realm of truth. It is apt to break its bounds and encroach upon its neighbours, and even upon those with whom it can hardly be said to have a natural affinity. It has indeed trespassed largely. Its province is not geology, or astronomy, or politics, or, even as a matter of jurisdiction, morality. It is not the office of religion to pronounce whether the sun moves or stands still. Nor does it follow that the Pope has authority in morals, even though we were to grant, what we need not be at the pains to grant or to deny, that he is supreme in matters of faith. He *might* have a lawful jurisdiction in faith without possessing any jurisdiction whatever in the sphere of morals. The domain of religious truth is primarily that which concerns things invisible and eternal, and it has to do with things of time and sense so far only as these are the visibility of things invisible. Surely things eternal, and whatever appertains thereto, are dominion enough, without the earthly mockery of a worldly throne or even of a philosopher's chair.

The fact is, that religion, to the detriment of truth in general, and to its own unspeakable loss in particular, may be said to have been engaged in minding everybody's business but its own. Its language might well be, "They made me the keeper of the vineyards, but mine own vineyard have I not kept." When the Church is finally stripped of what we may call its foreign and usurped possessions (a surrender which is continually, however unwillingly on its part, in progress), it will perforce, in its naked and destitute condition, turn its attention from the dross it has so unworthily coveted, to its own rich and imperfectly developed territories. The Church, when the buyers and sellers are finally whipped out of the Temple, will find the truth of what she has taught rather than practised, that the things which are seen are temporal, and therefore worth nothing, though they be thrones and dominions and principalities and powers; but that the things which are unseen are eternal, and therefore "worthy of all acceptation."

IX.—FAITH OR UNBELIEF IN ITSELF PROVES NOTHING.

If thy belief in Christianity proves that it is true, my unbelief proves equally that it is false. My unbelief as an argument is as good as thy faith. The truth is, faith or unbelief demonstrates nothing, one way or the other. Our beliefs are merely so many propositions to be put to the test, and to be ultimately accepted or rejected as they turn out to be true or false. Faith, in short, is not infallibility. It is the common assumption of all religions philosophically to assume faith to be certainty, and this prevailing tendency is as rife in Geneva as in Rome. The only difference is, that in Romanism this claim is gathered up and centred in one supreme Head, whereas in Protestantism it is myriad-headed, being parted into as many heads as there are individuals, or at least sects, in the whole body of Protestant Christendom. No wonder, then, that the religion of the present day, being self-made, is so sweet a morsel in the mouths of those who love rather what is sweetly false than what is bitterly true!

Thy first step in the path of true science, and in the ways of true religion and of true humility, is to believe firmly that what thou believest firmly may possibly prove false. Thou art a Christian man, and thou professest to believe with thy heart all the articles of the Christian faith, and thou accountest them therefore true. Well, so far as thy reason is sound, and thy honesty pure, and thy nature genuine, and thou art entirely free from prejudice, so far thy faith stands a corresponding chance of being what thou believest it to be; but so does also, on the same conditions, the faith of him who holds the exact contrary. What is to decide between him and thee? Assuredly not faith. Faith has given rise to hosts of controversies; when was it ever known to settle one? Nor is there any possibility of believer and non-believer, or of believers of varying form and colour, ever meeting together on common ground, and comparing notes to purpose, until they both of them hold as their first and great principle that what they respectively believe may possibly be false, and that there is need of a daysman between them.

And what is this daysman? We will not venture to say specifically; but it is some objectivity which thy thoughts and likings and prejudices shall have no control over, and to which both thy beliefs and those of thine adversary must unconditionally bow. Hitherto, it may be, thou hast been worshipping idols, the work of thy mind (or rather of thy likes and dislikes, for thy mind may have had little or nothing to do with the matter), but thou hast not found the true God; nor am I quite sure that thou hast yet begun in earnest "to seek after Him, if haply thou mightest find Him." When thou dost begin to seek, there is but one principle, and that is to put aside thyself, and to count thy faith at least as in suspense until it be ratified.

X.—FAITH UP TO A CERTAIN POINT GOOD; BEYOND THAT POINT, EVIL.

It is not in the nature of faith to bear the whole stress of religion. Faith, when we would put that burden upon it, breaks down, or turns to unbelief or superstition. Faith, which up to a certain point is one of the best things in the world, becomes, when it goes beyond that point, one of the worst, and chiefly because in this its non-natural stage it occupies a place which is not its own, and whereby it keeps out some higher and better thing. A superfluous faith occupies the place of a necessary knowledge.

XI.—FAITH MUST GO ON OR GO OFF; IT CANNOT STAND STILL.

Faith—that is to say, faith in things eternal, faith in God's revealed will—is a grand reality; but it is not a reality with which we can stand still and rest content; it is not a finality. Why not? Have I not the Bible? Have I not Moses and the Prophets, Christ and the Apostles? Why not be satisfied with hearing them? Why not rest content on that basis of Holy Scripture? Or I have my belief in the Church: why not be content with that foundation? For this simple reason, that it is out of our power to stop short at our original faith, even were we so minded.

Faith is in its very nature transitory, and not permanent. Faith must of necessity go on or go off. Faith must rise to knowledge, or sink to unbelief or superstition.

Nor would it be wisdom in us to rest satisfied with faith, even were it in our power to do so, seeing that we are permitted to go further and "add to our faith knowledge." If faith in the things of religion be good, a knowledge of these things must be far better. If the belief that God hears prayer comforts us and stirs us up to pray, is it not a higher consolation still if belief should become experience? We believe that Christ wrought miracles; but what is this belief compared with a possible experience of a miracle wrought upon ourselves or in connection with ourselves?

Nor would the Bible itself have us be so content with faith as not to seek to go further. Certainty, in some form or other is the mark towards which Holy Scripture would have the Christian ever press forward:

certainty of sight or certainty of knowledge, or what may amount to assurance of some kind. The blessedness of the pure in heart is that they shall "see God," not merely believe in Him. We are taught to pray that we may "know the love of Christ which passeth knowledge." "I know whom I have believed," is the exultant exclamation of the great Apostle—not merely, I believe in Him. And what is hope, but some better thing than faith as regards certainty? Hope is a substance, faith is a vision. Hope is a first-fruits, a pledge on the part of God of the truth and reality of that wherein we believe. Faith is a promise, hope is the partial fulfilment of the promise; or rather, faith is a belief in the promises of God, and hope is an earnest of the realization of those promises.

In a word, faith, according to the Bible, is good, very good, and absolutely necessary; but knowledge is better, far better. Not that all Christians, as a matter of course, go on from faith to knowledge. Not all that is called faith is faith. It is real faith only that ripens into knowledge. But real faith is a comparatively rare thing. The faith so-called of Christians in general is, for the most part, merely nominal. They take the truth of Christianity for granted, and call it faith. This merely nominal faith ends, as we might expect, where it began. That which has no beginning cannot well come to an end. It has no reality, and is consequently incapable of increase or decrease. No faith is so abiding as that which exists only in name. You cannot shake its foundation, for it has none.

It is such faith as this that our great poet seems to have had in his mind when he makes Camillo say of Leontes, in the *Winter's Tale:*

"You may as well
Forbid the sea for to obey the moon,
As or by oath remove or counsel shake
The fabric of his folly, whose foundation
Is piled upon his faith, and will continue
The standing of his body."

What Leontes had got without reason, reasons were powerless to move. But a real faith must go on, and its goal is knowledge or certainty of some kind. It is not a quagmire or a pool, but a stream of living water. Progress is the law of its existence. He who lives the life of faith must find eventually, whether he looks for this consummation or not, what this life of faith is; and if he is a man of reflection as well as of practical piety, he keeps this final result continually in view. He, on the other hand, who has no faith but in name, will wonder why to believe in the Bible or in the Church Catholic should not be all-sufficient; why, in short, the believer should not be content with simply believing and making a profession. Such contentment, however, is a mark, not of humility, but of indifference.

The problem which is the virtual title of these Thoughts, "How may I *know* that Christianity is true?" is not everybody's problem. It is a right inquiry, only it needs the right sort of inquirer; and the qualifications of this genuine seeker after truth in this particular matter are a living operative faith to begin with, and, over and above all, reflection brought to bear upon faith and its workings in our own individual experience. Faith may indeed rise to knowledge unconsciously to ourselves; but in order to take an interest in what we may call the science of religion, and to give others the benefit of our experience, we must not only be religious, but give good heed to what we experimentally find religion to be.

XII.—GALILEO A PATTERN TO THE BELIEVER AS TOUCHING HIS FAITH.

Galileo may be well taken as a pattern of the method the believer ought to pursue in putting his beliefs to the test; for just as Galileo was not satisfied with believing that the sun does really rise and set, though it appears to do so, but was resolved to bring the truth of this appearance to some unquestionable proof, and found that in this case seeming is not reality,—so the believer who is of such a mental constitution as not to confound belief and truth together, feels constrained to submit his beliefs to some test, if he can by any possibility do so, especially when he considers that truth in astronomy is but a shadow of the importance of truth in religion. He holds himself bound, in short, to try in some legitimate way to know, if possible, how far what he believes is true in religion. So far as we are content to be merely Christian believers, however hearty and honest we may be in our beliefs, what are we but followers of what we may call the Ptolemaic system of Christianity, taking things to be so because they seem to be so, and because the world generally holds them to be so?

XIII.—MAN NOT INDEBTED TO PHILOSOPHY FOR THE ELEMENTS OF RELIGION.

The religious sense in man, that is to say faith, is the origin of our primary religious ideas. So at least we have had reason to think. It is observation that tells us that this is their origin—observation brought to bear upon our natural faculties—such observation as is within the reach of all of us, provided only we have the power of reflection and will exercise that power, that is, the power of turning the eye of the mind back upon the thinker. What other origin could there be? What could philosophy do for us by the method of argumentation, with no eyes, but only a mind, though it may be a mind of no ordinary qualifications? Philosophy essays to speak, and does indeed seem to speak; but in reality its utterances are voiceless. All the efforts philosophy has made to find some better starting-point in religion than faith, have only proved to be so much labour well meant, but profitless.

Where is the philosophy which will undertake to prove, and not fail in the endeavour, the simplest and most fundamental proposition of all religion, that there is a God? Faith gives us at least a belief that there is a God. Well, that is something, and may, if properly husbanded, lead to a good deal more. What does philosophy do? It looks with an eye contemptuously askance at faith, but has nothing to put in its place. Philosophy is ambitious; it disdains faith, and will have nothing less than demonstration even to begin with. But whatever efforts philosophy has made to put religion on a basis of positive proof to start with, all these attempts, even according to the confession of philosophy itself, have ended where they began, except for the trouble and bitter disappointment they have invariably entailed.

In short, if man were without the spiritual

sense—that sense which we affirm for him whereby he believes, and only believes, that there is a God—he would be left literally "without God" in the world. "Through faith" (not through philosophy or metaphysics, or call it what you will) "we understand that the worlds were framed by the word of God." Philosophy, which rejects faith, has not succeeded in finding even a nominal substitute for faith. It scorns the confession embodied in the creeds; but neither will it put it within our reach to say, "I know." Tell philosophy you will at all events hold fast by your faith until it provides for you some better thing. Faith is at least something, with its single eye; philosophy is a blind man talking about colours.

XIV.—SUPPOSE PHILOSOPHY COULD GIVE US DEMONSTRATION, TO BEGIN WITH—WHAT THEN?

But suppose philosophy had succeeded in putting religion on a basis of demonstration, to begin with—what then? Suppose we could begin with saying, I know that there is a God, instead of merely, I believe in God—wherein should we be the better? Our theory, we confess, of faith as an independent faculty, would have been overthrown; and our occupation, so far as regards the purpose which these Thoughts are intended to serve, would be gone; but what else would not be gone too? A great deal more than our theory would have vanished; religion itself, in its very essence, would have come to nought. Philosophy, when fighting against faith, is fighting against religion itself. Religion is faith. But let religion be resolved into a proposition of Euclid, and be no longer faith, to begin with; let its first step be, I know, instead of, I believe; and it will then not only be true that you do not need faith as a starting-point in such a religion, but it will equally be true that you do not need faith at all from first to last. Faith is transcended at the very outset, and left behind for ever. Philosophy has borne you aloft to a higher region immediately on your setting out, where, instead of the confused but strong twilight of faith, you enjoy the full blaze of certainty. Religion has changed its nature, if, indeed, it has not ceased altogether to be.

XV.—THANKS TO PHILOSOPHY FOR ITS ENDEAVOURS, NEVERTHELESS.

Why, then, should not the believer at least be satisfied with simply believing, to begin with? Why should he be anxious to prove to demonstration, as a starting-point of his religion, that there is a God and a world beyond the grave? He would not get more, this Christian philosopher, for his pains; he would get less. Why the so-called infidel should deny that the elements of religion are capable of demonstration, we can well understand—he rejects religion altogether, and in every shape and form; but why the believer should strive after knowledge, to begin with, is not so easy to say. Why should he wish to supersede the eternal principle of faith as the basis and starting-point of all religion, and establish religion on a new principle of proof positive? Would he prefer to build the edifice of his Christianity on a mathematical foundation, and with mathematical framework, after the example of the Ethics of Spinoza? He would certainly, if he succeeded, prove more than he ever meant or desired to prove. He would destroy religion altogether.

In fact, it is no less the real interest of the believer than it is the supposed interest of the unbeliever, to hold that the being of God is not within the pale of demonstration. Philosophy has done religion at least this much service, that it has shown us what it cannot do for religion. This negative conclusion, that demonstration of the elementary truths of religion is an impossibility, is of the highest practical value. What all philosophy has failed to effect, must, we are sure, be in the nature of things unattainable. We see clearly in this universal failure that religion must be, to begin with, by faith or not at all. There is no competitor as against faith for the office of laying the first foundations of religion in the heart and mind.

XVI.—WHY ARE OUR RELIGIOUS IDEAS SO INDISTINCT? DIFFERENT CLASSES OR ORDERS OF IDEAS.

We can hardly, however, after all, be surprised at the attempt being made to apprehend more clearly than we do the things that are outside the conditions of time and space, supposing there to be any such realities. These supernatural objects are by no means so distinct as we should wish, or indeed expect them to be. Might we not have anticipated that the ideas of God and of eternity would be simply overpowering;

that they would assuredly not be the faint images in our minds we find them to be; that they would at least be such as no one could deny the existence of? Faint we confess them to be subjectively; but this sort of dimness or insufficiency proves nothing against their objective reality. Ideas are real, not in proportion to their vividness, but their power, as we shall perhaps more fully perceive if we try to distinguish the principal classes or orders of ideas.

In the first place, those ideas are clearest of all which the mind forms for itself, of which it is creator and consequently master, and which represent nothing in the universe objectively; those ideas, in fact, which could be nothing at all were they not ideas. What ideas could be more clear than those of Shakspeare when they were in his own mind, and when he had not yet set them before the eyes of men? What ideas could be more sharply defined than those on which mathematical science rests, the idea of a point, a line, a triangle? and yet these things are purely a creation of the mind: there is no such thing *in rerum naturâ* as a triangle, nor even a circle in the pure mathematical sense, certainly not a mathematical line, "length without breadth," least of all a point, "neither length, breadth, nor thickness." These ideas are purely the creation of the mathematical faculty, and they are unsurpassable in clearness. But what power has the science of mathematics, with all its lucidity of idea, to move men practically this way or that? Whom has the irrefragable truth that "the three angles of a triangle are equal to two right-angles," ever consoled in misfortune or disquieted in his worldly success? Mathematical ideas, while they are clearest of all, are at the same time practically weakest.

Next in order, perhaps, are what we may call practical ideas, or ideas of time and sense. Our ideas of an objective world, of the things we touch, hear and see, are not so clearly defined as our ideas of a square or of a circle, but they are more real than these purely mathematical ideas; not absolutely real, but still we are practically satisfied of the reality of the things they represent, and of revolutions on this ground we have heard and may hear continually. The veriest idealistic philosopher would, as a man of plain sense, whatever he might do as an idealist, be perfectly content if he were to have a landed estate or a bag of gold on the basis of such evidence. He would raise no objection whatever on the score of the idealistic presentment not being so satisfactory as it might be imagined to be.

There is a third order of ideas, and the one indeed with which we have more immediately to do. The dimmest and most obscure ideas of all, and yet the strongest infinitely in their effects, are our religious ideas. They lie at the very root of our nature. They constitute the basis of our being. When they move in force, they set in motion the whole man. They upset governments, they overturn kingdoms, they change the face of the world. They are the volcanos and earthquakes of human nature and of human society. They dissolve old associations, they form new brotherhoods. "The father is divided against the son, and the son against the father; the mother against the daughter, and the daughter against the mother." They are the most hidden, and at the same time the most powerful, elements of our being. You may deny the existence of religion, and question what it is; you cannot, however, doubt the effects which the name of Religion (reality or unreality) always has produced in the world and in the individual, and which there is no sign whatever it will not continue to produce to the end of time; and it is in these effects of religious ideas, not in the vividness or otherwise of the ideas themselves, that their reality consists. Dim and indistinct our religious ideas undoubtedly are, but this is only so much as to say that faith, which is the strongest power in the world and the most effectual, is at the same time the most deeply hidden and the least cognizable of all the forces of human nature.

No objection, therefore, can rightly be urged against faith as a faculty, on the ground that the ideas which are the expression of this faculty are mystical and, materially speaking, shadowy, and not, as perhaps we should have thought they ought to be, bright and precise. We have no right to expect them to be mathematically clear and distinct. What we are entitled to look for is, that things invisible and infinite, if they are brought to bear at all upon the finite things of time and sense, would have an overwhelming influence upon these finite things, and so by experience we find it to be.

XVII.—WAS A REVELATION NECESSARY TO MAN?

Why has God given man a revelation at all? or why not less or more, or in a different way? Why just what we have and as we have it? Suppose "holy men" had never spoken, had never been "moved by the Holy Ghost"—what then? What if man had been left entirely to those primary religious beliefs that are in man? Would he ever have risen from belief to knowledge? Would he (without revelation) have grown in religion as he does (without revelation) in literature and art and science?

XVIII.—WE MAY AT LEAST IMAGINE A REVELATION NOT NECESSARY.

It is at least not beyond the power of imagination to conceive that man might thus have made progress in the ways of religion. We can suppose him reasoning thus with himself: The God in whom, however faintly, I believe, must be good and take a pleasure in goodness. He will, I cannot doubt, stand by those who look to Him for guidance and protection. "He will not suffer the righteous to fall for ever."

What can that invisible world be, of which I have also a conception and for which I yearn, but a world of righteousness, and therefore of happiness? What can it be but the blessed abode of those who have walked upon earth in accordance with the precepts which I find written upon my heart and mind? God has not left me without a sense of His presence altogether. I do not see Him with my bodily eye, it is true; but I do feel that "in Him I live and move and have my being." I fail to understand myself else. What is His design, but that I should make the most of this His witness within me? Let me only be faithful in little, and He will make that little much; and in process of time He will give me to rejoice in a clearer and better light, and finally in the light that is now unapproachable. What can this dark world, in which my lot is cast in a way inscrutable to me, and which I find to be my place of sojourn but for a brief and uncertain period, and not my home—what can it be but my school, my training-ground, my place of trial, to the end that it may be proved what manner of man I am, whither my inclinations tend, and what my dispositions are; and not only so, but that I may be made meet to be a partaker of that higher and better state of existence towards which my being aspires?

In some such reflections as these a man might naturally be supposed to hold converse with himself, even without a special illumination from on high in the way of revelation. And he would, as a matter of course, walk accordingly. He is a man of faith, and he would live by faith. He could not do otherwise if his faith is genuine, and we take it to be so. He lives according to the light of his inner man—what follows? His conclusions will put his premisses to the test, and try the validity of them. He has lived in the conviction that there is a God and another world—what has he found?

Any confirmation of his beliefs? Or has his faith been put to confusion? He has "sought after God if haply he might find Him"— have his seekings been altogether fruitless, or have they been attended with results, outwardly and inwardly, which he felt he had a right to expect, and which, in a measure at least, would give rest to his soul? This finding or not finding, this fruit or no fruit of his seeking after God, would show whether his hypothesis that there is a God was well grounded or not, at least in the only way in which it was possible for him to put this matter to the proof.

The man who lives as though there were a God, even though he be left entirely to the light of nature, must eventually have his creed ratified or destroyed, strengthened at least or weakened, if he can afford to wait long enough, and work earnestly enough. In this way we might represent to ourselves one who believes in the two fundamental truths of all religion—the being of a God and the reality of a future world—to work out for himself the problem of religious evidences, and to set the truth of religion, if true, upon a sure foundation, so far as he was individually concerned, independently of a revelation from Heaven, whether Christian or Jewish or any other. The work would doubtless be an infinitely hard one on these bare conditions, harder by far than is the solution of the same problem with the aids which revelation affords; but still we are not authorized in pronouncing it to be utterly impossible of accomplishment.

XIX.—BUT FACT DOES NOT CONFIRM OUR IMAGININGS.

So we might conceive; but how far does the history of the world as to religion justify our theorizings? Happily or unhappily for our theory, man has been left to himself, and these the very best of men, in larger or smaller measure, and under a variety of circumstances, so far as to show what he can do, at least what he will do, in the way of religion, if not assisted specially from on high; and what says experience? The result of all experiments of the kind is not such as to warrant any sanguine expectations we might have entertained as to the value of man's unassisted powers in the sphere of religion.

That unique people, the Greeks, the world's wonder in art and philosophy and learning of all kinds, were left to themselves and to the light of nature in their religion—what was the result? Are the Greeks of the year 80 before the Christian era more religious than were their forefathers of the year 800 B.C.? Were they more God-fearing when Paul preached at Athens on Mars' Hill, than in the heroic days of Homer and Hesiod? Is not a steady and continuous decline observable in their morals and in their religion, generation after generation, until it reaches a point, both in morals and religion, below which it would not be easy to fall?

And what shall we say of the Romans? The word religion (*religio*) is their word. Did this *religio* flourish more and more in this its native home as time went on, or did it turn to corruption, and end at last in utter decay and the vilest superstitions? The ancestors of the Romans were, according to Sallust, "religiosissumi mortales"— what were they in the days of Sallust himself? So far from the term *religio* acquiring a richer and deeper significance as time passed by, it lost more and more its pristine virtue, till at length it more than vanished altogether.

How, finally, stands the case concerning even the Jews, with their partial revelation, as compared with the non-revelation of the Gentile world? When prophecy ceased, as it did some centuries before the birth of Christ, and they were left to themselves in this respect, what became of them? Did they rise religiously, so as more than to retain their ancient vitality, or did they decline? What are they during the interval between the Old and New Testaments? Do they grow in spiritual wisdom and grace, or is there a melancholy declension? They are certainly not more religious in the days of Scribes and Pharisees, than they had been, for example, in the latter time of the Babylonish Captivity, under (if we may speak of a prophet as we do of a king) Isaiah II. For the 500 or 600 years immediately preceding the advent of the Redeemer, they are left in a great measure to the sacred records of past generations; there is neither prophet nor open vision for the greater part of that wilderness period of Jewish history; and the consequence is that true religion, at the expiration of those dreary days, has turned absolutely to corruption. When the Apostle Paul wrote his first chapters of the Epistle to the Romans, there was little to choose, in point of religion and morality, between Jew and Gentile.

The case of the Jews seems to show that not only is revelation necessary if man is to grow in religion, but revelation up to a certain point, inasmuch as we see that the partial revelation accorded to the Jew was insufficient to counteract the forces in human nature which are persistently drawing man in a downward direction. So we find that, while we have no difficulty at all in *imagining* man to be religious and even to increase in godliness without revelation, and with the aid which nature alone may be supposed to afford, experience, so far as the appeal to experience is open to us, whether Grecian, or Roman, or even Jewish, is very far from justifying these anticipations.

XX.—WHY THIS DISCREPANCY BETWEEN IMAGINATION AND FACT?

Why this marked difference between what we should have expected and what we actually find by experience? Can it be that we have left out of our calculation, in our suppositions as to what might have happened under certain circumstances, some important factor in the reckoning which we ought to have taken account of? So, indeed, it is. We have been asking unconsciously what the world might be expected to do when at its best, and when consisting exclusively or mainly of well-disposed individuals, instead of taking man as he is. Imagination makes very light of practical difficulties, and the obstacle in the present case is that most formidable one of man's own nature, which tends not heavenward, and which cannot be said to love truth. "Men love darkness rather than light," it is never to be forgotten. So far from taking pains to know the truth, and "searching for her as for hid treasure," they will hardly stoop down and pick the truth up when it lies before them on the ground. Were man but enamoured of the truth, the imagination we have indulged in might at some time and somewhere have realized itself.

But man is not fond of truth, least of all of heavenly truths. Men love pleasure, and riches, and honour, and books, and pictures, and art, and literature; but they cannot be said to love truth for its own sake. They like to make-believe that they have a regard for it; and what they prefer most of all is to appear to follow the truth, when in reality they hold truth in leash, in order to let it slip at the right moment for their own purposes. We are happy, and even ostentatiously proud, to go with the truth, so long as the truth happens to go our way; but when truth will do this no longer, then it is clearly seen whether truth all this while has been really leading or only following. Woe worth the truth if it presumes to take the lead and expects us to follow! If we would rightly conjecture what the world is likely to do in any given case, we must take mankind at a very low average, and consider, not what this or that good man, who is in goodness much beyond the ordinary run of his fellows, may be expected to do, but what the world will probably do as a whole; and if we would hit the mark, we must take care to aim low enough.

There are, we know, men of whom it may be truly said that they love light rather than darkness, and whose unceasing endeavour is light-wards. A world of light-loving men might possibly work out the problem of truth in religion on the condition of no revelation from on high, but not a world of men such as we actually find mankind to be. Lessing, in his *Erziehung des Menschengeschlechts*, does indeed not hesitate to express the opinion that man might have succeeded in finding truth in religion without the assistance of revelation, only give him time enough. He does not, however, compute how much time would have been needed, how many millions of years, or what might not have happened meanwhile—

whether mankind, through the corruptions that are in the world, might not have perished outright before the momentous experiment had been completed. A world of Lessings might possibly have succeeded in doing the work of religion without revelation, but hardly the sort of world with which we have experimentally to do, a world which finds it apparently much easier and more agreeable to fabricate a religion in its own image and likeness, than observingly and patiently to inquire whether there be not somewhere, and to be found by some means, a religion which is not altogether of man's device.

XXI.—MAN NOT LEFT TO HIMSELF AS REGARDS RELIGIOUS LIGHT.

But man has not been left to himself, and to what is called the light of nature, in the matter of religion. God could not indeed have thus left the world partially, or almost entirely, in the dark, though man so left might have been able, even under these unfavourable conditions, somehow or at some indefinite time, to "work out his own salvation." "God giveth to all men liberally," and His gifts in revelation are no exception. It is not the divine principle to give us as little as we can possibly do with, but as much as ever will be for our good. The Giver of all good things does not closely calculate how little man can do with at the very least, but how much will be for his good at the very most. On this principle of infinite liberality it is that God has given His revelation of divine truth.

XXII.—BUT HAS GOD GIVEN US AS MUCH AS POSSIBLE?

But has God really done so? Is it the simple fact that He has given us the utmost in the way of revelation that could have been of service to us? Could not more have been done, and would not this larger measure have been so much the more for our good?

If revelation is a good thing, we could hardly, it might be urged, have too much of it. The world is not over-religious as it is: would it not have been helpful to us religiously, if the Almighty had vouchsafed to us some more convincing proofs of the truth of religion than we now possess, proofs which it would have been impossible for the unbeliever to evade or explain away?

XXIII.—TO HAVE GIVEN MORE WOULD HAVE BEEN HURTFUL, NOT HELPFUL.

To speak plainly, it would not have been of advantage to us that we should have had a revelation in any respect of a more cogent character than we possess now; assuredly not that we should have one of an absolutely compulsory character. Most good things are only good to a certain extent and in a particular way. Just as "There is some soul of goodness in things evil," so also there are possibilities of evil in things good. A revelation might be so good as to destroy the very purpose and end of revelation itself. Those more convincing proofs which we are tempted to ask for would have been a violation of that principle of faith, according to which God has given His revelation. Man is a free agent, and revelation a free agency, and works on the will and affections; and a larger measure of revelation, that is to say, a revelation of a compulsory character (for such it must of necessity be), and which should act more on our fears and less upon our affections, would have been a revelation more or less destructive of both freedom and revelation.

Religion is of faith, and faith is of free-will. In whatever other respects a man may be bound, he is free as to his faith. Whatever appeals to my faith leaves me free to take my own way, the way that I judge best. But suppose the truth put so plainly as to necessitate my going as a man of any sense at all in a particular direction—where is then my freedom? The moment you make the truth of revelation as good as certain, religion is forced upon me; it is no longer any test of the real bent of my mind. What I do is no longer any evidence of what I wish to be, but of what I am compelled to be.

On this condition of maintaining strictly the principle of faith, the Author of man's salvation has gone as far in the way of spiritual help as we may presume it was possible for Him to go. More would not have been more, but less. The only further appeal practicable would be, not to faith, but to sight—would be a breaking down of the wall of partition that separates the two worlds, a rending of the veil, an actual vision of those eternal verities which are ours now only by faith so far as they are ours at all. The effect would be to weaken or destroy the relation in which man now stands to the Gospel; we should be no longer Christians on the ground of preference, as we are now, but of necessity; we should be God's bondmen, not His sons or even His servants.

This, whatever else it might be, would not be religion as we understand it.

Suppose the Almighty were to vouchsafe us but a glimpse of that other world in which we now must be content only to believe—of its eternal glories on the one hand, and of its blackness of darkness on the other—what would become of our voluntary service? How could it be known, with these certain evidences of the truth of Christianity before us, whether we served God from fear or from love? The whole character of religion would be changed, or rather religion itself would vanish. What had been so far "the glorious liberty of the children of God," would now be a mere phrase, or rather a base and inglorious slavery. Religion is, on its present conditions, "a discerner of the thoughts and intents of the heart;" it declares plainly whether we love God or not; but what would it be, if its evidence were put beyond doubt, but a vile hypocrisy, or, if we prefer the name, a calculating prudence? One thing is certain—it would not bear the marks of an honourable service. We now believe because we wish to believe, for faith is of the heart; we should then believe, if believing it could be called, because we had no option but to believe.

Dives, in the parable of the "Rich Man and Lazarus," prays Father Abraham to send Lazarus to his five brethren, "lest they also come to that place of torment." Abraham refuses; such a messenger, he says, for such a purpose would be superfluous; "they have Moses and the prophets, let them hear them." Dives is not satisfied; he still presses his suit. One from the dead, an actual vision, not a thing to be believed merely, but a thing actually seen, would be a stronger argument, he urges, than even Moses and all the prophets. Abraham's final rejoinder is peremptory and absolute: "If they hear not Moses and the prophets, neither will they be persuaded though one rose from the dead." The stress is on the word "persuaded;" as much as to say that whatever argument is put forward in the name of religion, if it keeps not mainly within the limits of persuasion, oversteps its legitimate boundaries. The apparition of Lazarus to the five brethren, whatever effect it might produce, could not be of a persuasive character, and that is decisive as to at least its inutility. Like the ghost in *Hamlet*, it might make a purely momentary impression, operative while the ghost was present, and gone when the ghost was gone, or it might even be "a damned ghost." Whatever the effect might be, it would not be of such a nature as to affect the heart or move the will, and leave the subject of its influences all the while free. In short, God's revelation never, it would seem, transgresses the boundary which separates between persuasion and compulsion. The apostle Paul was right well aware of this principle. "Knowing the terrors of the Lord," he says, "we persuade men;" we do not terrify them; the effect would be evil and not good.

However strange it may seem that the world of spirits (on the supposition of such a world) should be so entirely "the undiscovered country from whose bourne no traveller returns," as to give us no certain information concerning itself, this strangeness will altogether disappear if we will only reflect that revelation is essentially of faith, and that an actual visitant from this unknown world would act injuriously upon this cardinal principle of religion itself; that it would either have no influence at all upon our faith (it would have had none upon the faith of the five brethren, the parable says), or the effect might be prejudicial, if not destructive of faith altogether. So far as we allow the principle of faith, and the sanctity and inviolability of the principle, we must, upon reflection, admit that a break for the most part of all inter-communion of a visible character between the world of sight and the world of things invisible, can be no argument against the existence and reality of an unseen world—nay, that the impenetrability of the veil as regards the many is an absolutely necessary condition, if there is to be a veil at all.

XXIV.—WANTED A METHOD BY WHICH RELIGION MAY BE TRIED.

How may I *know* that Christianity is true? Find me a METHOD. My present position is that of a believer, but I am not at all content with that position. Besides, what men call believing is, generally speaking, little more than taking as a matter of course the thing in which they say they believe, as though it were self-evident and needed no further proof. In this way the Mussulman or Hindoo believes. The consequence is that, his religion not in any way resting upon reasons, reasons cannot move it. Are we to take for granted that we are all right? We cannot at least do that. Give me, then, I say, a method, a rule, by which I may try my religion whether it be true or false, and, incidentally, all other religions that are or ever were. It is an enviable state of things, no doubt, to be able to solve the truth of our religion by the easy and self-flattering method of assuming its truth to begin with, but it is not a reasonable thing. We are, in religion, under what we may call the Ptolemaic system. Where is Copernicus? And when I ask for a method, I mean that and nothing more. I do not wish you to apply this method for me, and prove to me what Christianity is one way or the other; you cannot do that; I must, I am aware, apply it for myself. A method, and a method only, is what I want.

But let me be precise as to what it is I really expect. I wish to find out, not whether religion merely is true—that would be an easy matter comparatively—but whether Christianity is true. Christianity is religion with a difference. Christianity is not only a belief in God and in an invisible world—for these are the elements of all religions—but it consists besides of certain historical facts, which are said to have taken place upon this earth 1800 years ago. Are these things so? I might be a religious man, and not a believer in these particular facts; in other words, I might be a holder of the great fundamental truths of all religions, and yet not a Christian. Is it true that Christ, the Messiah, the Son of God, was crucified; and not only crucified, but that he rose again from the dead, and ascended up on high, and gave the gift of the Spirit? Are these things so? I do believe them and with all my heart; but how may I be assured that my belief is well founded? Give me a method by which I may know, and not merely believe, that Christianity in particular, and not merely religion in general, is true.

XXV.—A SCIENTIFIC METHOD POSSIBLE.

Is it possible to put Christianity on a scientific basis? It is possible; the materials are at hand, with all needful appliances. Faith furnishes the materials: in the first place, the materials common to all religions, viz. the being of God and a spiritual world; and secondly, the materials which are contained in the Christian creeds and in Holy Scripture generally, and it may be elsewhere, and which are peculiar to the Christian religion. But this basis of faith is not yet a scientific basis, nor in itself qualified to be so. Science means certainty, not merely belief. The question to be asked, therefore, is, How may I *know* (not merely believe) that Christianity is true? How is this to be compassed? By means of experience. The end of religion is man made good, perfectly good, and therefore perfectly happy. So religion professes. Is it as good as its word? So far as its professions are made good, so far religion is true; so far as they are realized in us, so far our religion is true.

Faith and experience are thus both of them necessary to determine truth in religion: faith wherewith to provide all requisite materials, and without which no religion, nor even a conception of religion, would be possible; and experience, in order to confirm these materials, and so stamp them with an imperishable value. Such a method may rightly be termed scientific, if, indeed, it be science to distinguish satisfactorily, in things of a particular character, between what is true and what is false.

So a science of religion is a possibility, on two admissions: first, that man has a faculty which takes cognizance of the things of religion—of those things, that is, which are beyond the bounds of things material—a faculty which we call the faculty of faith, and by which we not only mean the act of believing, but the believing faculty itself; and secondly, that he has the means of bringing his beliefs to the test of experience, so that they remain no longer beliefs merely, but rise to the height of ascertained facts. If our system were not according to faith, it would not be religion; if it be not ratified by that which alone in all practical things has the power of ratification, that is, by experience, it is not science; but resting, as our method does, on *both* faith and experience, it professes to be religion made science, or a science of religion.

XXVI.—EXPERIENCE THE TEST OF TRUTH IN RELIGION.

What I affirm, and would repeat again and again, is, that whatever truth there be in religion of a practical character is to be found by experience, and by experience only, and is equally discoverable by the unlearned and the learned; and that each believer may in a measure ascertain this truth for himself. What we believe is not necessarily true, however firmly we believe it. A test is necessary. If no proof were possible, then one religion would be as good as another, and religion would be altogether, what it is in no small degree now a mere matter of fancy.

What do we ourselves find religion to be? That is the vital question. Why is not this test universally applied? Are men really in earnest as to religious truth? What course can be more conclusive and simple? We come in faith; what do we go away with? The sick and needy came to Christ in faith when he tabernacled with men, and they found the faith they had brought with them confirmed—nay, put beyond doubt. Had they experienced nothing, they would have gone away with nothing, not even with the faith they had brought with them. What find we now-a-days? Does experience justify our faith or condemn it? But do we even look for a reality? Remember, if you do not look for a reality, you do not get it, though God be ready to give it. And remember, that to look for this blessing aright means to look earnestly and unto the end. "Though it tarry, wait for it; because it will surely come, it will not tarry" (Hab. ii. 3). It may be late, but it will not be too late.

XXVII.—FAITH AND EXPERIENCE THE TWO PILLARS ON WHICH CHRISTIANITY RESTS.

The two pillars on which, from a scientific point of view, Christianity rests, are faith and experience. We begin with "I believe" (where indeed everything begins), and we end with "I know" (where also everything ends), unless, indeed, our pursuit in the realm of religious inquiry has proved barren and unfruitful. Be careful to keep these two poles of thought asunder, and each in its own place. We say there *is a God*, when all we can mean, if we would speak exactly, is that we *believe* there is a God. What is our belief worth in itself? Just nothing whatever, unless it be ultimately confirmed by experience. Or do we mean to imply that we are infallible? We do imply this, whether we intend it or not, if we regard our faith as an evidence of truth absolutely; and this self-infallibility it is which is at the root of the many confusions there are in religion, whether practically or scientifically considered ; and, we might add, not in religion only, but in common life, and even in philosophy.

XXVIII.—THE THREE STAGES OF RELIGION: 1. FAITH; 2. WORKS; 3. EXPERIENCE.

Religion has three stages. The first stage is faith. We believe that there is a God and a world beyond the grave, or we do not. We believe in revelation, or we do not. We believe all the articles of the Christian faith, or we do not. How we came to these beliefs matters little. Why we believe or do not believe is not in our power to say. Faith is elementary, and not Q. E. D. The next stage is a life in accordance with our beliefs. A man's life always is, if he really has a faith, in keeping with his faith. It is not so much what we *think* we believe, or what we *say* we believe, as what we *do* and the kind of life we live, that is to be taken as the true and certain index of our faith. So, at least, says that not least of thinkers, Descartes (*Quelques règles de la morale*): "Pour savoir quelles étaient veritablement leurs opinions je devais plutôt prendre garde à ce qu'ils pratiquaient qu'à ce qu'ils disaient.... car l'action de la pensée par laquelle on *croit* une chose étant differente de celle par laquelle *on connait* qu'on la croit, elles sont souvent l'une sans l'autre." However this may be, unless we practise what we believe, our first stage is the only stage, our faith becoming corrupt or vanishing entirely.

Our third and last stage is the experience of whatever kind, good or bad, which this life of faith brings, negativing or confirming our expectations. We believed that certain things were true, that they would produce certain good results; we walked in the way of these beliefs, and so put them to the test. What have we found? Has experience ratified the things in which we believed, or not? If so, we now know what, to begin with, we only believed. We now are fully apprised of the infinity or nothingness of our beliefs. We *shall* know, on the supposition of a world to come, at all events in that future world. Then, at least, our faith will rise to, or rather be merged in, certainty.

But have we not a right to expect that we shall enjoy that experience to some extent "now in the time of this mortal life," if we are believers indeed and faithful unto the end? Is it not simply an impossibility that one should live the life of faith, and remain a mere believer unto the end? This belief must ripen into knowledge, or die out altogether, or turn to unbelief, or perchance be lost in superstition or mysticism. The only healthy development of faith is that it should become certainty. Wherein this certainty will consist, or to what it will amount, we do not profess to explain; but that faith, as the consummation of a life of faith, will either die out, or live a new and higher life amounting to assurance of some kind, seems clear from the subjective nature of faith itself.

The last stage, in fact, of a good man's life is Christian experience, which puts him in a position to say, not merely I believe, but, in a measure, I know that these things are so. And it is the aggregate of these experiences that may be said to constitute in the strictest sense evidences of Christianity. Evidences of Christianity are not to be expected to begin with; they ought to be forthcoming to end with. You have lived the Christian life in all godliness and sincerity; what have you found as the sum and substance of your long and toilsome journey through this world's wilderness, now at last when the river only separates between you and the heavenly Canaan? Tell us, now. Such knowledge is of a very high order, the highest possible in this life, and pity 'tis we have not more of this practical and satisfying sort of evidence.

At any rate, do not fail to make plain to

your own self what you find in this life's pilgrimage; for remember that if you would more than believe that what you believe is true, you must solve this problem for yourself, and that the three practical stages of which we have spoken are the only conceivable method. You will never be able to read out, or think out, the truths of religion, or so much as the being of a God. The only practicable way of arriving at truth in religion is to work it out. The problem of religion is a practical one, and one which, in fact, all who are believers indeed do work out for themselves, though it may be for the most part unconsciously. Unfortunately, a so-called Christian experience, even when it is forthcoming, is mostly of a subjective character and of doubtful value. What we lack is objectivity.

XXIX.—CHRISTIAN SCIENCE NOT IN ITSELF RELIGION.

Is this science of which we have been speaking absolutely necessary to a life of practical religion? By no means; for if so, what judgment are we to pass on all the religion of the world up to the present time, which undoubtedly has intellectually been anything but scientific? Christian science is not in itself religion, notwithstanding that it is concerned about the things of religion. A scientific knowledge of religion is not of direct value religiously, but only intellectually. A man may be practically a religious man, without troubling himself about a science of religion; as, in fact, very few religious people do so concern themselves, or, indeed, know how. To care for the science of religion, as well as for religion itself, a man must be something more than religious, he must be scientifically gifted as well—a two-fold inner endowment not always to be met with in the same individual. Just as in the cultivation of the ground the husbandman may plough and sow, and gather in the fruits of the earth, and enjoy all the bounties of earth and sky, without for one moment concerning himself about either geological or astronomical science, so it is with religion.

A man may do his practical work, as a man of faith and "doer of the word," without ever asking himself what faith is, or how it stands in relation to knowledge; as also, on the other hand, it is quite possible for a man to argue unexceptionally as to the evidences of religion, and at the same time not to be himself a religious man. When such a one talks about the evidences of religion simply as evidences, and not as religion, and thereupon proceeds to expatiate as to what evidences may rightly be expected, it is quite possible he may be talking reason and be deserving of attention, though he does not care about religion. He may be prejudiced against religion, just as we may be prepossessed in its favour; but his arguments may have weight, nevertheless. It is not indispensable, in order to discourse sensibly on this subject, that he be a religious man, but only a man of sense.

Only there is this difference, that none but a man who first cares somewhat for religion can go on to care for its truth or otherwise. The presumption is that when an individual even quarrels with religion, he is not altogether indifferent to it in itself. He may proclaim aloud that he is not a believer, and all the while he may be a believer unconsciously to himself, if, indeed, the faculty with which we believe, and the faculty by which we know that we believe, are (as Descartes says) not one and the same. He may have interrogated his intellect and found no faith there (as, indeed, we never do find faith in the intellect); but he has not properly searched his heart, or perhaps he would have found at least so much faith there as to account for his troubling himself about religion at all.

But however these things may be, and whatever effect a science of religion might have on religion itself as a whole, we content ourselves here with remarking that we consider the problem of these Thoughts to be, in its direct intention and effect, an intellectual and not a religious one—as science applied to religion, and not as religion itself; though what it might prove to be indirectly as to religion it is impossible to foresee. The probability is that the gain would not be inconsiderable. To enlighten the mind, especially as to religion—what is it but to quicken the whole man, morals and religion included? Though the intellect is not the heart, they are in closest connection and sympathy.

XXX.—EXPERIENCE NO NEW TEST OF TRUTH IN RELIGION.

In bringing religion to the test of experience, we do not profess to be devising some new thing. This appeal to experience is everywhere implicitly and explicitly contained in the Bible itself—nay, it is a test which lies in the very nature of all religion. Christianity in particular claims our allegiance as "worthy of all acceptation" on the ground of its "many great and precious promises," the fulfilment of which is not deferred exclusively to the life beyond the grave, but is in part, and by way of foretaste and earnest, to be realized in this world, and so may be appealed to as evidence of the truth of Christianity now. How far do these Gospel promises come true? How far are they (as they are said to be) "Yea and Amen to every one that believeth"?

Herein lies essentially the appeal to experience, which decides for all practical purposes how far any religion whatsoever is "worthy of all acceptation," whether it be Islam or Hindooism or Judaism or Christianity itself. A religion which makes no promises, is a vain and empty thing, not to say a deception. A religion which does not make its promises good, is a religion which has forfeited its credit. The believer, as a matter of course, looks for the fulfilment of these promises. "I have waited for thy salvation, O Lord!" is his language in prayer and patience. Supposing him to find the promises made good which he regards as of God, in what has he been engaged but in applying instinctively and unconsciously the test of experience to his faith? So we, in this our method, are not inventing some hitherto unheard-of thing. We are simply following the path which every believer must take in his Christian course, according to the very nature of the case.

The only point that is new is, that we are bringing reflection to bear upon this old and necessary method, and for purposes of scientific investigation. We always did, as we needs must so far as we were Christians at all, walk in this way of experience; but now we are doing so with the clearly defined purpose of satisfying ourselves as to what experience has to say for or against the path we are practically pursuing. Just indeed as if, in things pertaining to man's body, a physiologist should eat, not from the ordinary motives only on account of which men naturally take food, for health and strength or to appease appetite, but with the set purpose of ascertaining experimentally the laws of nutrition and digestion; so also we, in precisely the same way, are inquiring into the laws of the religious life in answer to the query, What good is there in religion? We live exactly as other Christians live, only we are engaged in taking meanwhile observations by the way, which our fellow-christians are not supposed to take.

And what a pity that this matter of scientific observation is not kept more prominently in view in what are called Christian biographies! These biographies are professedly a record of Christian experience. How far do they answer their professed design? The phrase, Christian experience, or similar phraseology, is met with in them in all due frequency—how far are they in deed what they are in word? The so-called experience is too frequently of an altogether unpractical and purely subjective character, consisting for the most part of that phase of Christian experience—if it can be called experience—which is emotional, and therefore fluctuating and uncertain.

What we look for in Christian biography (and so seldom, if ever, get), is the experience of those who are of the reasonable rather than the emotional type. We say "rather than," because no one is purely emotional or purely rational in his nature, and therefore not in his religion. We are all mixed characters, more or less, in these respects. What we need—if we may call it so—is objective evidence rather than subjective, seeing and knowing rather than feeling—such an experience as is beyond the reach of self-deception. You are at the close of your earthly pilgrimage; you have lived the Christian life all your days, faithfully and perseveringly; you are a man of reason, a man of reflection; you have brought these qualities to bear upon your religion—what have you found? You must be in a position to give us at least one word on this head of a solid and trustworthy character. For what purpose indeed should a Christian biography ever be written, but to that end which the godly Psalmist puts before us (lxvi. 14), "Come and hear, all ye that fear God, and I will declare what He hath done for my soul"?

XXXI.—WHY HAS SO SIMPLE A METHOD NOT BEEN UNIVERSALLY FOLLOWED?

But how is it that this method, if it be so simple, has not been acknowledged and formally acted upon long ago; especially when we consider that the matter is so weighty? Chiefly for this very reason, that the matter is of such weight, and because truth is irksome, and, to say the least, not universally courted and followed. Do not suppose that truth has but to show itself in its own beautiful form, to be embraced and loyally obeyed. Truth is not attractive to the world at large. It is unsightliness to the untruthful; "wisdom and goodness to the vile seem vile." What says the highest authority of all?—"Men love darkness rather than light, because their deeds are evil" (John iii. 19). Lord Bacon's words are to the same effect. "What doth bring lies into favour," he says in his *Essay on Truth*, "is a natural though corrupt love of the lie itself." Aristotle is more charitable, if we are unwilling to say less discerning: "The difficulty of discovering truth," he says (*Met.* ii. 1), "lies not only in the things themselves, but in us; for as the eyes of bats are to the light of day, so is our mind to those things which are by nature clearest of all." In other words, truth, to say the least of it, is too strong for man's weak vision. It needs a veil to cover its countenance—like Moses when he came down from the Mount—if we are to look it steadily in the face. It must be diluted or tempered with alloy before it will pass current.

But whatever the cause or causes may be, truth does, as a matter of fact, move most painfully and sluggishly along the path of scientific progress. The science of geology or astronomy or medicine would, historically considered, afford a curious and melancholy commentary on the words, "Men love darkness rather than light." But the kind of truth which makes slowest progress, if, indeed, any at all, is that which is most important of all—moral and religious truth; and for this very reason, that such truth concerns our interests most. Why bad men should not seek after that truth which, were it found, would be their condemnation, or why they should not welcome it when they cannot avoid acknowledging it, we have no difficulty in understanding.

But it is not bad men only who do not embrace heartily the truth; good men—aye, even the best of men (or those who pass for being so)—are more than indifferent where we should rather have expected a warm welcome. How do we account for this hostile or at least cold attitude? For one thing, as we have said, if not the great thing, it is not every man that has any great love of the truth for its own sake. We follow it, so far as it suits our purposes of self-interest, or credit with our neighbours, or even our curiosity; and then we part company with it as soon as ever it will no longer go our way. If truth is on the side of our religion, we hail it enthusiastically as a valuable ally, and rejoice in the light of its countenance, and make every use of it (it will at all events impose upon others); but if the truth is against us, we put it on one side, of course as quietly and considerately as possible, yet without the least compunction.

But besides having no great love of the truth, it would appear that we have no great confidence in it either. It must be kept in hand, and under some kind of restraint. It cannot safely be allowed to do just what it will. We know not what it might do if left to itself. We are, therefore, highly circumspect in our dealings with it, lest it might unexpectedly take a turn which might greatly embarrass us. Truth shall not be our master, but our humble servant only. Few men indeed have reliance enough upon truth (religious men in general have little or none) to cast in their lot with it, come what will, or so much solid confidence in their religious beliefs as to bring them to the test of truth if at any time an opportunity should offer.

Moreover, men in the dark can do what they list, and call their deeds by what name they please (such men literally "love darkness"); whereas when in the light we are under some necessity of speaking and acting as things are, and not altogether as we wish them to be. "Truth," to cite Lord Bacon once more, "imposeth on men's thoughts," and men do not like their thoughts to be imposed upon; they prefer to impose upon truth, and to think what they like, not what they must, and to put truth itself under constraint, rather than be in any way in bondage themselves.

Now in that doubt and uncertainty in which we find ourselves as to religious truth, antecedently to experience, having merely the dim and flickering light of faith at best as a guide, the believer is in a measure a law to himself; he does what he likes, and calls it religion. His religion is consequently human, and only so far divine as its divinity may happen to fall in with this prevailing human element. Let only the light of truth enter our minds, and we are forthwith under a necessity of calling things by their right names. The barriers of our pride and self-will and self-worship, the least amiable features of our nature, are broken down, and we are henceforth subjects, willingly or unwillingly, where we have hitherto lorded it as supreme.

Besides, we must remember that in the matter of our religion we are all of us more or less committed beforehand to particular views and opinions. Our prestige is at stake, and in its tenderest point, for a man's religion is the man himself. Truth makes sad havoc of views and opinions where they are not found to rest upon a solid basis. What, indeed, might not happen to our Catholicism or Protestantism, to our High Church or Low Church or Dissent, if some infallible test of the truth of our special phase of

Christianity could only be at once and rigidly applied?

But we are in no overweening haste to precipitate any such decision. We prefer, on the whole, to remain as we are. We have shrewd reasons for wishing to do so, even though these reasons be deeply hidden, rather than on the surface. We at least hold a position from which our adversaries so far have found it impossible to dislodge us, though we on our side are equally unsuccessful against them. What the impartial intervention of truth might effect it is hard to say; but we partly suspect what the result might be, and we would rather not force a judgment, which, though it might confound our foes, might also roll us in the dust indiscriminately with them. We know what we are now, but what we might be we know not, were we to submit ourselves and our religion unconditionally to the stern arbitrament of truth.

The simplicity, therefore, of our method

cannot upon reflection be regarded as an argument against its validity. It is not any difficulty in the method that makes against its applicability, but rather its profound distastefulness. Truth is bitter; and if we have not found it so, it is possible we are under a mistake in supposing that we have found it at all. Perhaps our method might have been more acceptable had it been really difficult, that is, obscure and involved, instead of its being so very plain and imperative.

XXXII.—BUT IS THERE NO METHOD ACTUALLY AT WORK NOW?

But is there no method or system of any kind at work now for arriving at truth in religion without resorting to this method? A system there may have been—nay, must have been; but has it been the true one? "By their fruits shall ye know them." A true method is an infallible instrument for the discovery and furtherance of truth, and the marks of this method are certainty, progress and unity. What certainty is there in religion in the present day, philosophically (or even religiously) speaking? To what extent are we able to say, This is or this is not, and not merely I believe this or I believe that? Where is progress? Is it not our pride and our endeavour to go back to the elements and beginning of things religious, rather than go on to perfection, as though truth lay behind us in religion, and not before us? And lastly and chiefly, Where is unity? But this is a question we will not even ask. One consolation we have at least in putting forward these Thoughts, and that is, that we cannot possibly do any mischief. It is out of our power to be destructive, for there is nothing of a progressive or certain or harmonious character for us to destroy. There is a method already philosophically in religion, but it is an astrology, not an astronomy.

XXXIII.—DIFFERENCE BETWEEN THEOLOGICAL AND SCIENTIFIC METHOD.

What is the difference between the method of arriving at Christian truth set forth in these Thoughts, and the method which has been actually at work, consciously or unconsciously, in the Christian Church from the beginning? The difference is this, that in Christian theology faith of itself is regarded as a complete foundation; and on this foundation of faith alone is built intellectually the whole fabric of what is termed theology, or the science of religion—the whole structure, in short, of Christian evidences—with what fruits time has shown, and time, if we mistake not, so long as the system continues, cannot fail still more conclusively to prove.

The method of these Thoughts, while it leaves faith its rightful place and acknowledges its function, and indeed magnifies its office, insists upon faith in all cases being put to some test before it can be regarded as truth, or serve as a foundation for any structure of Christian theology properly so called. Faith alone, cries Theology, is all we need in any way as a basis of Christian truth, or as superstructure either; faith, when properly safeguarded and rightly embodied, will bear any weight of truth you can put upon it. Not so, say these Thoughts, not faith alone, but faith and experience hand-in-hand—faith seconded by experience, and so made perfect. You may believe provisionally just what reason and inclination may prompt, only you must not stop short there; you must put your beliefs to some test and prove them to be true, before you are entitled to speak of them as truths or to proceed upon them as such.

And it is a consideration worthy of notice from a practical point of view, as regards what is called the science of theology as hitherto understood and professed, that a man may, without religion or even morality, cultivate this kind of science; he need not be himself a religious or even a moral man to follow this pursuit. On the other hand, one grand recommendation of our method practically is, that a man must first be a religious man, and, as religion presupposes morality, also a moral man, before he can take up the science of religion on our lines to any purpose, or can hope to make any way, even the least, in the prosecution of religious truth. Whatever our method may be intellectually, it is at least in the most rigid sense of the term *a moral method.* A bad man cannot follow the system set forth in these Thoughts.

XXXIV.—DESCARTES NOT WITH US IN OUR METHOD.

We have not Descartes with us, it must be confessed, in this our method—that is, if we understand him aright where he says, "Les choses qui nous ont été révélées par Dieu sont les plus certaines de toutes nos

connaisances, puisque la foi qu'on a en elles
.... est un acte non de l'esprit, mais de la
volonté." What can this mean? That
what I believe is a certainty because I believe it—in other words, I am endowed with
infallibility? and further, that what I will
is a certainty because I will to believe it—
in other words, my will is arbiter of right
and wrong? Is this what is meant? If so,
Descartes is undoubtedly not with us. Nor
do we much wonder: he could hardly be
with us and with the Catholic Church;
and Descartes, though a philosopher and a
genuine lover of truth, was unquestionably
a prudent man.

What this philosopher says, however, of
the science in general of his day, must be
acknowledged to hold good of the theology
of our own day or of any day: "Toute la
science que nous pouvons désirer, fût-elle
renfermée dans les livres, cependant ce qu'ils
ont de bien se trouve mêlé à tant de choses
inutiles et dispersé dans une masse de si

vastes volumes, qu'il nous faudrait, pour les lire, plus de temps que **la vie humaine ne nous en fournit**, et de **plus grands efforts** d'esprit pour **en extraire les** choses utiles qu'il n'est besoin pour les trouver de nous-mêmes." **These** remarks, if applied to theology, **are as much as to** say that if **you wish for** the truth that **is** in theology, **it** will take you less time and trouble to make it out for yourself than **to** ascertain it from the bulky and multitudinous tomes of divinity that **are in** existence. **So we** think; and on this principle **we** have presumed **to act.**

XXXV.—WHAT A SCIENCE OF RELIGION IS NOT.
(M. EMILE BURNOUF.)

Nor have we with us M. Emile Burnouf (*La Science des Religions*, 1870): "**Ce n'est à la science**," says this writer, "**d'examiner la valeur absolue des religions.**" But is not this precisely what the peculiar province of religious science is, viz. **to** distinguish sharply and absolutely between the true and the false in religion? That this is its great duty, the author himself acknowledges (p. 276): "La théorie d'Agni est-elle vraie absolument?" He, however, nowhere seems to feel himself called upon to give an answer. Again, he remarks that the science of religion "n'a rien d'aggressif." Poor Religion! if it is not to be aggressive, when everybody else and everything else is so. Is not all science aggressive? Is not the science of astronomy aggressive? Where is now the Ptolemaic system? Nay, has not science made war upon religion—righteous war perhaps, but still war? What has become of the sun that in bygone days stood still on Gibeon, or of the creation of the world in six statute days? Religious science is bound to be aggressive, if only in self-defence; for none are so little peaceful themselves as the so-called votaries of science.

Religion, it must be remembered, is fast losing what may be termed its foreign—

perhaps we might even say, its usurped—possessions, and is in danger of losing even its own rightful territory, if it does not at least assume manfully the defensive. So long as science was not yet, religion stood confessedly at the head of all truth, by virtue of the greater excellence of the material with which it has to do; but now that truth in so many departments of human inquiry is made science, an unscientific religion contends with science at every disadvantage; it is virtually defenceless.

If the truth must be said, a science of religion which does not regard it as one of its primary duties to maintain its defences where it has right on its side, and to be at least in that sense aggressive, will soon have no religion to defend. Altogether, M. Burnouf's book, notwithstanding what you might expect from its title, is not a science of religion. It is for the most part a collection of facts, more or less connected with religion, and that is all. You might, with just as good reason and as good results, bring together all the alchemics that ever were, and call the compound a science of chemistry, as say of M. Burnouf's volume that it is a science of religion.

This author's science of religion would seem to proceed upon the principle that all things that are called religion—or are believed to be such, no matter by whom—are equally religion scientifically considered. He takes whatever facts of religion may present themselves, just as they come in his way, and from this indiscriminate budget of data draws his conclusions; not, however, that there is much of a conclusion. If, indeed, as he appears to think, all the great religions of the world are only so many reforms in religion, or at least so many advances upon a former and less perfect stage of development — Buddhism, Zoroastrism, Mohammedanism, Christianity — would it not seem rather to follow that whatever is in religion is false, or at least imperfect, and that we are only in some preparatory state still, and no more justified in constructing a science of religion out of the materials at our disposal, taking them just as they are, without having first submitted them to some test, than we should be warranted in fabricating a science of geology out of the first chapters of the book of Genesis and similar materials?

Does it not, in fact, simply follow from M. Burnouf's position, that while man must have a religion of some kind, however rudimentary may be his system, he has not yet hit upon the right method of discriminating between true and false in religion, or between that which is relevant and to the purpose, and that which must be cast aside as a worn-out garment? When he does find truth in religion, one of the first things he will do will be to draw a sharp line between what he knows and what he only believes—a very difficult task (simple as it may be thought to be), at least for those whose minds are rather of the religious than of the scientific order. Most of the facts of religion as hitherto understood he will find to be facts of mere opinion rather than facts of experience. M. Burnouf's book is in many respects an example of what a science of religion ought not to be.

XXXVI.—ORTHODOXY AND THESE THOUGHTS.

What have we to do with orthodoxy in connection with these Thoughts? Properly speaking, nothing whatever. Do we oppose it? No; but the truth is, it does not lie in our path according to the principles laid down for ourselves. In the first place, orthodoxy deals with natures and essences; we, with facts, with things and persons as they appear to be, with phenomena rather than with noumena. Secondly, orthodoxy determines truth by means of a majority, be it of a particular or general council; not the best way of arriving at truth even in things not appertaining to religion, and certainly not an infallible one in matters of religion; we are neither majority nor minority, being only a single individual. But chiefly, orthodoxy arrives at truth by the easy method of speculation and disputation; we are bound to work out our problems practically, and this is not always easy.

In a word, a science of dogma such as is in vogue, and a science of practical religion such as these Thoughts endeavour to establish, go in different directions and rest upon different foundations—orthodoxy, upon faith alone; and science, upon faith and experience combined; that is to say, we do not admit faith as a foundation until it has been first tested and ratified by experience. By what means shall we determine the nature of the Deity? He is Three and One. How can these things be? We conceive that any such problem, however imposing in itself, is out of our line. We believe it, and there we stop; we do not argue. It is a metaphysical question, and we are practical.

Besides, we consider that we can serve God without metaphysically attempting (for we should never succeed) to understand His nature, just as we can take our food and be nourished therewith, and all the while be ignorant of the nature both of the food and of him who feeds thereon. Are we not, therefore, more than justified in confining ourselves entirely to the practical side of religion? And, by the way, are we sure that this practical mode of procedure is not after all the path by which we scale those hitherto untrodden heights which metaphysical speculation has so far attempted in vain? "The secret of the Lord is with them that fear Him, and He will show them His covenant" (Ps. xxv. 14). That is to say, the way of practical religion is the only way to a knowledge of God's secret things.

For these reasons and for other kindred considerations, he is the truly religious man who keeps to the strictly practical path in religion, and eschews speculation as a vain and empty thing at best. If any one will not walk in this obvious path, what is his alternative? Can his eye pierce a thick and three-fold veil? If not, let him not vainly imagine that he can apprehend either the nature of man or the nature of God, or what is "within the veil," unless it shall please God to draw aside the covering for a brief space, or supernaturally to open his eyes. Consequently we are not in these Thoughts speculative or metaphysical; we are simply practical.

XXXVII.—SPECULATION NO WAY TO CHRISTIAN TRUTH. FOUR REASONS.

On what grounds do we affirm that it is not possible to find Christian truth, not even so much as the being of a God or the reality of an unseen world, by any unpractical way —by the way, that is, of metaphysics or speculation?

(1) In all probability the things of that world of spirits differ *in their nature* from

the things of this world of sense, this material world; so that it is impossible to argue from the latter, the only kind of world we are acquainted with, to the former.

(2) Even though the two worlds with which we have to do were of the same nature, we are not justified in concluding from what is here to what is there. It would be possible to make a tolerable conjecture as to what is in the next room, though we may never have been in it; but it would only be a conjecture, it would not be a certainty. If I really wish to know, I am not satisfied with supposition or argument of any sort, but I enter the room and see, if I may be permitted to do so, or, as the next best thing, procure trustworthy information as to the contents of that other room. Just so as regards what may be in the next world, which we call the world of spirits (though we have not the slightest conception as to what spirit is, only we presume it is not matter), unless we can

open some channel of communication, our thinkings and distractions of mind are all "vanity and vexation of spirit." Speculating will do absolutely no good; believing will do good, but only as a preliminary step and to a certain extent.

(3) What has speculation ever effected? Men have speculated and metaphysicized, from Thales to Aristotle, from Aristotle to Descartes, from Descartes to Kant, from Kant to the latest philosopher of all, whoever he may be—and with what result? Is there a God? They cannot one of them say for certain. One affirms and the other denies, and we strike a balance of argument, and in conclusion we are just where we were when we began. The whole argumentation may be represented by the formula, $1 - 1 = 0$. The scales are exactly even.

(4) If speculation is a possible way to religious knowledge—that is, if man, by the exercise of his own natural faculties, can find out God and the things of eternity—

what need of revelation, or faith in revelation? We need no Bible in that case, with its word of prophecy, to tell us what to believe—the word of philosophy is sufficient; we put aside faith as unnecessary and superfluous, and at one bound, by means of philosophy, arrive at knowledge. In brief, the net result of speculation in matters of religion is scepticism—that is to say, an evenly-balanced conclusion for and against the essentials of religious truth. To this goal speculation leads you, and there it leaves you; there is no road forward; the only road open to you is backward, to begin again where you began before, with the same weary round and the like profitless result. The game of metaphysics — the players being equal—is invariably a drawn game. You are unable to conclude as a matter of reasoning that there is a God; you are equally powerless to show for a certainty that there is not a God—a plain proof that in metaphysics believer and unbeliever alike have their labour for their pains. If you would know whether there is really a world of spirits, go and see (as, indeed, you will one day go, if there is truth in religion); or apply some test, if you cannot yet go. To sit still and think merely, and then to write down what you think, is simply that "making many books" of which *the preacher* declares "there is no end," and in which there is assuredly no profit.

XXXVIII.—BISHOP BUTLER AS TO THE WORTH OF SPECULATION IN RELIGION.

"Religion," says the Bishop in direct terms, "*is a practical thing*"—which is as much as to say, unless we are mistaken, that it is not speculative. His exact words are (*Charge to the Clergy of Durham*, 1751): "Besides, as to religion in general, it is a practical thing, and no otherwise a matter of speculation than common prudence in the management of our worldly affairs is so. And if one were endeavouring to bring a plain man to be more careful with regard to this last, it would be thought a strange method of doing it to perplex him with stating formally the several objections which men of gaiety or speculation have made against prudence, and the advantages which they pleasantly tell us folly has over it, though one could answer those objections ever so fully."

This is a noteworthy saying, and all the more so as coming from so noteworthy a man in the domain of metaphysics. It is as much as to say that, when you play with religion, you speculate; when you come to be in earnest, you cast speculation to the winds, and no more speculate than you do in respect of your food or in the performance of your every-day round of duties. Speculation, in short, he says, has neither more nor less to do with religion than it has with the ordinary affairs of life. Speculation, however, we must add, is not absolutely nothing, if we would strike a fair balance of relative good and evil. (1) It is a fascinating exercise of the mind. (2) It gives you an opportunity of having to do with religion intellectually, while at the same time holding aloof, it may be, both heart and strength. (3) It enables you to frame objections against religion. (4) It gives you the power at the same time of meeting those and all other objections. (5) It leaves you just where you were when you began to speculate—neither better nor worse.

These and the like advantages speculation affords. But there are two things it has not in its power to do for you in the least degree: it neither tends to make you religious as to the heart, nor helps you to the conviction that religion is true as to the mind. It gives your heart nothing; it gives your mind nothing. Speculation is the shadow of religion, not the substance. Take to it by all means if you are so minded, until you find it can do nothing for you; and when you have worked it out and played it out, you will, if you are wise, leave it for ever. You will at least have learnt what is not the road to Christian truth.

Truth in all practical things—the greatest as well as the smallest, the smallest no less than the greatest—is determined by one and the same method: you conjecture or believe to begin with, and you arrive at certainty to end with, if you persevere as you began. You may eschew this common method as long as you like, but you are sure to be brought down—it may be on your knees—before it at last, supposing you to be in earnest, as we have a right to suppose. You will then have learnt that the only way of truth is not the lofty one of speculation, but the lowly one of a good life. You may think too much.

XXXIX.—HUMAN KNOWLEDGE RELATIVE, NOT ABSOLUTE.

Man has to do with things, not absolutely, but relatively. Objects do not appear, you say, as they are, and I have to find out what they are. But can you do so, and is there any necessity? You allow that they appear as they are *intended* to appear. They therefore appear relatively to us as they are. With what they are absolutely, we have nothing to do, unless we also were ourselves absolute. Hence the distinction between phenomena and noumena would seem practically to vanish. In our thinkings, therefore, we must draw the line strictly on this side what we call the absolute. It is true in philosophy as in religion that there are "secret things" which "belong unto the Lord." Besides, how do we know that, as regards the finite things with which we have to do, there is any difference between appearance and reality?

XL.—THE BIBLE: ITS PROPER PLACE IN THE CHRISTIAN SCHEME.

When religion is lowest in the heart, then it is found that Scripture stands highest in our esteem. He who is too poor to afford a new coat, will perhaps be thankful for the gift of a second-hand garment. The Bible is God's Word to us at second-hand. Moses or Samuel or Noah had God's Word at first-hand. So it is possible we might have it, if we would only not dictate to the Almighty through what channels He shall speak, or when He shall cease speaking. But we have presumed to lay down laws for the Almighty, both as to what He shall say and when He shall stop. First of all, our language is, taking the Bible in our hands: This is God's Word in the highest possible degree, if not in the only possible way; then we shut the Book, and cry, Enough! God shall say no more. Everything depends upon putting even good things in their right places, otherwise even good things become bad things. What is the legitimate place of the Bible? Not that of supreme arbiter in matters of religion, from which there shall be no appeal. At least, we are right in affirming that this is not the position which the Bible has invariably without exception held from the beginning. It gradually grew to this infallibility.

One example may suffice to prove this at all events non-invariability, and this one example we take from the Commentary on the Four Gospels by Euthymius Zigabenus, a monk of the twelfth century. "The best thing," he says, "is that we should not need help from Scripture at all. We ought to be so pure in life as not to require the outwardly and visibly written book. Then shall our hearts be inscribed by the Spirit, just as a book is written with ink. But since we have forfeited this grace of the Spirit, we shall do well to avail ourselves of the *next best thing*, and of necessity make use of the Bible. God spake to Noah and Abraham and their posterity in the old dispensation, also to Job and Moses, not through the medium of writing; but as He found their minds to be pure, He spake to them personally and directly. But when the whole people of the Hebrews had corrupted themselves, then came tablets and letters and writings. So also as regards the writers of the New Testament. God did not give the apostles any Scripture, but instead of Scripture He promised them the grace of the Spirit. That the Spirit is better, hear what the prophet says (Jer. xxxi. 31—33): 'Behold the days come, saith the Lord, that I will make a new covenant with the house of Israel and with the house of Jacob. Not according to the covenant which I made with their fathers, but this shall be the covenant: I will put my law in their inward parts, and will write it in their hearts.' Paul also upholds this excellence when he says (2 Cor. iii. 3): 'Ye are the epistle of Christ ministered by us, written not with ink, but with the Spirit of the living God; not in tables of stone, but in fleshy tables of the heart.' But when in process of time men went wrong—some in doctrine, some in life and manners—the putting in mind which books afford was found to be needful. Consider, therefore, how great an evil it is if we—whose hearts ought to be so pure as not to require even Scripture—not only come down from that high place, but do not even care to avail ourselves of this second-best assistance, neglecting even the Scriptures themselves as of no value." Thus far Euthymius Zigabenus. If we are not at one with this monk of the twelfth century as to the proper place of Holy Scripture in the Christian scheme, is it that we are sounder in faith in this matter, or less so, than he?

XLI.—THE BIBLE RESTS UPON CHRISTIAN EXPERIENCE, NOT VICE VERSA.

Are Christ's miracles true? Were they ever really wrought? Do you experience miracles? If not, what good to you though Christ's miracles be all true? On the other hand, if you do experience miracles, or at least are satisfied with your experience altogether, what harm to you though Christ's miracles be, as some pretend, so many myths? In other words, the truth of the Bible rests upon Christian experience, not Christian experience upon the Bible. So long as thou art merely a believer, thou restest upon Scripture; when thou "comest, in the unity of the faith and of the knowledge of the Son of God, unto a perfect man, unto the measure of the stature of the fulness of Christ," thou art emancipated from the letter, and Scripture rests so far forth upon thee. The man in whom no miracle shall ever be wrought is a lost man, and he who expects none is a losing man. What is to raise thee from the dead? Thou wilt die: what is to restore thee to life again? The miracles of the Bible will not save thee, however heartily thou accept them. What thou standest in need of is, not the mere record of a miracle, but the miracle itself.

XLII.—THE RIGHT WAY OF DEALING WITH HOLY SCRIPTURE.

There are two ways of dealing with Holy Scripture. The one is to regard it, before ever you have opened the book, as pure and unadulterated truth—every chapter of it, every verse, every word. The other is, not to take the truth of the Bible for granted, not a single word of it, whatever your inmost thought or inclination may be, but calmly to set about the inquiry with the Bereans as to how far these things are so. The former of these methods is easy and flattering to self; it is indeed a tacit assumption of self-infallibility; the latter is hard and humiliating, and involves that, to certain minds, most unpalatable admission, that we cannot possibly say what is in a book until we have read it. Which of these two ways is, from a religious point of view, the more likely to be the right principle of dealing with a book which comes to us as from God—the proud and self-sufficient way, or the path of humility? From the religious point of view, we repeat; for as to the way of criticism or common sense, there never was or could be the shadow of a doubt. Unquestionably the method that exhibits all the tokens of modesty and moderation is the right way: so much so, that, were there any doubt as to the verdict of reason, religion itself—yea, even the Bible as a whole when properly interrogated—would turn the scale effectually against taking even the Bible for granted, to begin with.

XLIII.—RELIGION DOES NOT REST UPON BIBLE OR CHURCH AS A FOUNDATION.

When a good Protestant makes it his solace and his glory that his religion rests upon the Bible, what does he mean? What he really implies, if he will examine himself, is, that his religion rests, not upon the Bible immediately, but upon *his belief in* the

Bible—in other words, upon himself, for his belief is himself—in other words again, upon his own infallibility; for has he not pronounced the Bible to be infallibly true, and who is entitled to do this but an infallible man? "The less is blessed of the better," and he in this case is the better. This good Protestant first blesses the Bible, and then accepts it in consequence of this blessing. In like manner, when a good Romanist assures us that his religion rests, not upon the Bible, but upon his Church—"I believe in the Church"—what does he mean? Only substitute Church for Bible, and you have what must be his meaning, whether he thinks it or not. His Church blesses him, but he has first blessed his Church, so as to infuse into it that virtue which now enwraps him and makes him religiously confident. What a marvellous, and we may say self-satisfying, power of self-deception there is in this frail humanity of ours! You first, of your mere act and deed, invest a book or a church with infallibility, and this infallibility bestows upon you its blessing. Just as it was in the olden days, the days of idolatry, you first fashion your idol, and then fall down to worship the work of your own hands. Besides, we must never forget that what is lawful in Christianity is allowable philosophically to the same extent in any other religion; and that, if it is right for us to take the truth, even the infallibility, of our Bible for granted, it is equally right for the Mussulman to take the infallibility of his Bible—that is, the Koran—for granted.

XLIV.—THE BIBLE ITSELF COUNTENANCES A SIGN IN CONFIRMATION OF ITS WORD.

Whosoever refuses to take the Bible for granted and without inquiry, may successfully appeal to the Bible itself in justification of his hesitancy. The case of Gideon is conclusive on this head. Gideon has a revelation from heaven. The angel of the Lord appears to him. The injunction is laid upon him to save Israel from the hand of Midian. Gideon requires a sign whereby he may be assured that the vision is true, and that the Lord has really given him this commission. The sign he himself proposes is vouchsafed. The dew is on the fleece only, and all the earth around is dry. He is not yet fully satisfied. The dew on the fleece might possibly be otherwise accounted for than as a sign from God at Gideon's instance. He now asks that the sign may be reversed, that it this time be dry on the fleece only, and that there be dew on all the earth around. The Lord is not angry with Gideon, as Gideon seems almost to have apprehended. The second sign is granted, and Gideon is now satisfied that the Lord has really appeared to him and commissioned him to the war against Midian.

Are we wrong in following Gideon's example in the matter of the revelation made to us in the Bible? Nay, have we not twice

Gideon's motives? Gideon was sure up to a certain point. He was confident that an impression had been made on his mind, and that he *thought* he saw a vision, and that he *thought* also that he heard words out of the mouth of the angel that appeared to him. He had no doubt that in all this he was not acting the part of a self-deceiver. The only point on which he could possibly be in doubt was, as to whether he was not himself deceived, as to whether that of which he was subjectively certain was also objectively true. But we are not even assured as to this subjective certainty in the minds of those through whom we have the revelations of the Bible.

Were the revelations which are put on record in the Bible ever really made to those whose names they bear? Indeed, for the most part, they are without the voucher even of a name. In this respect, Gideon had an advantage over us. He was sure as to himself and his own honesty. He was sure "he *thought* he saw a vision." He might be deceived, but he was certainly not a self-deceiver. We are more than justified, therefore, in following the example of Gideon, and asking for some sign whereby we may know whether these things are of God or not. And what is the sign we naturally ask? The sign of God's Word fulfilled in us, in obedience to His command and for our good. When Gideon had overcome the Midianites, he needed no further sign; he had his sign to the full, a better sign than even the appearance of the angel. So when we, to our own good, experience the truth of what is written in Holy Scripture, having walked in the ways of the Word of God, then in truth are we fully assured that the Bible is indeed God's Word.

Not to rest satisfied without such a sign is a proof, not of want of faith in God, but of want of faith in man, and in ourselves especially; in other words, is a proof of humility. Gideon was self-distrustful. So ought we to be. So is the true prophet ever. Had prophets always a sign? Spinoza is of opinion that they had (*Tract. Theo. Pol.*): "Quamvis Scriptura non semper signi mentionem faciat, credendum tamen est prophetas semper signum habuisse." If prophets, with their higher spiritual intelligence, always had a sign, much more is it imperative that we should have some objective evidence sooner or later of the reality of God's Word to us.

XLV.—TRUTH OF BIBLE A CONCLUSION, NOT A PREMISS.

The religion of A.D. 1888 rests not upon the Bible, but, vice versâ, the Bible rests upon the religion of A.D. 1888. Paradoxical, but true. The foundations of religion, so far as our knowledge is concerned, lie not in time past, but in time present. To argue from the Bible to ourselves is to conclude from the unknown to the known, which is unprofitable even where possible.

The necessary order is to proceed from what we know to what we do not know. If I argue from Holy Scripture to myself, I necessarily begin with taking Holy Scripture for granted, which proceeding is just the opposite of science, however much it may be in accordance with the principles of what goes under the name of that which is the opposite of science.

Science takes nothing for granted but that which contains its truth in itself. If I reason from time present, I begin with indisputable facts, and so, at any rate, have a sure foundation, if only I can build thereon. In short, the truth of the Bible is, practically speaking, a conclusion, and not a premiss. What if I do not find religion to be true, now and to me? Can the Bible make my religion to be of any worth in opposition to my own personal experience? Would it be even any consolation to me to know under such circumstances that the Bible is true? But if I find religion to be to me all that I care to find it, now, personally, then the truth of the Bible follows, and from no other possible premiss.

Besides, we must always bear in mind that Christianity might have been true 1800 years ago, and may not be true now. Do we not hold, rightly or wrongly, that Judaism, which was once a living faith, is now dead or superseded as a religion? The Bible *was* true, therefore my religion which rests upon it *is* true, is an argument which is much more of a conclusion than a premiss. A living religion now, proves all that is of any value concerning the past, even though it leaves the past, it may be, considerably in the dark; whereas a living religion in time past proves nothing whatever concerning time present, or nothing to any practical purpose.

XLVI.—MORALITY AND RELIGION, HOW RELATED. RELIGION IS THE HANDMAID, NOT THE MISTRESS, OF MORALITY.

When you ask whether is greater, religion or morality, what religion do you mean—Christianity or Buddhism, or some other? Perhaps, as you are a Christian, you would reply, if you were to speak what you really think, that Christianity is greater than morality, but that morality is greater than any other religion.

Morality was before Christianity, and will be after Christianity, "when the Son also himself shall be subject unto Him that put all things under Him, that God may be all in all" (1 Cor. xv. 28).

Morality is the beginning of man's goodness, morality is the end; and Christ's religion is the means, and the only means, to that end.

"Alles was ausser dem guten Lebenswandel der Mensch noch thun zu konnen vermeynt um Gott wohlgefällig zu werden, ist blosser Religionswahn und Afterdienst Gottes" (Kant).

However imperfect morality may be without religion, religion, we must bear in mind, is nothing at all without morality. They are essential to each other, and it is hard to say whether of the two has the best of the bargain.

Christianity is the "leaven which a woman took and hid in three measures of meal until the whole was leavened" (Matt. xiii. 33); and man's moral nature is "the three measures of meal."

Which of the two is greater, morality or religion? Morality is greater than religion. We are to be "perfect as our Father which is in heaven is perfect;" and God is moral, not religious.

Religion is a means to an end, and that end is morality in the grandest and widest sense. How far does your religion conduce to this end? So far only is it true. "If any man among you seem to be religious, and bridleth not his tongue (which is a moral duty), but deceiveth his own heart, that man's religion is vain" (James i. 26).

"He hath showed thee, O man, what is good; and what doth the Lord require of thee, but to do justly, and to love mercy, and to walk humbly with thy God?" (Micah vi. 8).

"Think not that I am come to destroy the law or the prophets: I am not come to destroy, but to fulfil. For verily I say unto you, Till heaven and earth pass, one jot or one tittle shall in no wise pass from the law, till all be fulfilled" (Matt. v. 17, 18).

"But if ye had known what that meaneth,

I will have mercy and not sacrifice (morality and not religion), ye would not have condemned the guiltless" (Matt. xii. 7).

"Who gave himself for us that he might redeem us from all iniquity, and purify unto himself a peculiar people zealous of good works" (Tit. ii. 14).

"Hear the word of the Lord, ye rulers of Sodom; give ear unto the law of our God, ye people of Gomorrah. To what purpose is the multitude of your sacrifices unto me? .... Bring no more vain oblations; incense is an abomination unto me; the new moons and sabbaths, the calling of assemblies, I cannot away with. .... Your new moons and your appointed feasts my soul hateth. .... Yea, when ye make many prayers, I will not hear: your hands are full of blood" (Isaiah i. 10—15).

XLVII.—MORALITY: ITS END AND ITS AIM.

The end of morals is happiness; the aim of morals is virtue. The Epicureans made happiness the aim of life—an impossible aim, seeing that we know not, prior to experience, wherein happiness consists. How, then, can it be our mark? The Stoics, on the other hand, made virtue the end of life as well as the aim, virtue being to them its own reward—a noble sentiment, were it only practicable. Virtue may be misery; and how can misery be a reward? A prison or a block may be, and often is, virtue; but it is only a philosophy of words without feeling that could regard either of them as the reward of virtue.

The Epicureans were right in making happiness the end of life, provided only we rightly understand what happiness is; but they were wrong in regarding it as the direct aim of man. The Stoics, on the other hand, were right, so far as they made virtue the mark to be kept constantly in view; but they were wrong in holding it to be its own end. Virtue is a means to an end, but not the end absolutely. The Stoics merged happiness in virtue; the Epicureans lost sight of virtue in happiness. Who were right, and who were wrong? Both were right, and both were wrong.

Put the two together, and you have a perfect system of morals. Let Epicurus and Zeno join hands. Make virtue in all things thy aim, and believe that thou wilt attain to happiness in the end if thou strictly pursue the path of virtue. Righteousness in morals, as in religion, is by faith. What, indeed, is not by faith to begin with?

XLVIII.—MAN HAS MORAL SENSES OR FACULTIES TO BEGIN WITH.

Man has the power of distinguishing between good and evil. Whence this power? Is it in man to begin with—a moral sense, what we may call an intuitive or inborn faculty—or is it acquired? If we say that it is acquired, how do we know that it is so, unless we are able to look back to a time in the development of human nature when man was as yet destitute of the power of making these moral distinctions; or, indeed, not only to look back, but even to point out when and how the human family first became possessed of this faculty? But no such past time is within our ken, cast our recollection as far back as we may. These ethical distinctions have their roots and expressions in the origins of all languages, which is the same thing as to say that they are at least coeval with the origin of man as a thinking and sentient being.

They are therefore, so to speak, innate; they are an integral and inseparable element of our original constitution. They were born with us and in us. Nor, indeed, do we see how experience could have originated them. Experience may and does improve man, but it certainly never gives him being, either in general or in particular.

We are far of course from asserting that experience exercises no influence upon morals. It has a great influence upon morals; only it did not give birth to morals. We are not in any way indebted to experience for our primary moral perceptions. Experience never gave us what we call a *sense* of shame, or any sense at all. To say that a man has learnt morals from experience, or in any way independently of a moral faculty to begin with, is as much as to affirm that he has learnt to see without eyes, and that experience gave him his eyes. We learnt morals just as we learnt to walk. We had moral legs to begin with.

XLIX.—RELIGION AND MORALS DISTINCT, THOUGH CONNECTED.

Religion and morals, however closely connected, are nevertheless in the abstract distinct. As a matter of fact we find them to be so. A man may be moral, and at the same time not at all religious. Religion and morals may be found in every possible combination and dissociation. Jacob was religious, not moral. Esau was moral, not religious. Abraham was both moral and religious. Cain was neither. We shall readily understand how these two sides of one common goodness may be independent (though at the same time interdependent), if we reflect that the distinctive characteristic of morals, that which makes morals, is the moral sense, and the distinctive characteristic of religion, that which makes religion, is the religious sense, and that these two senses do not necessarily accompany or imply each other. Experience of course, as a test of truth, is common to both.

L.—MORALITY INCOMPLETE IN ITSELF AS A PRACTICAL GOODNESS.

Morality as a practical goodness does not complete itself. It falls short in all practical respects of the glorious end it aims at. The end of morality is man made perfect—perfectly good, and, by consequence, perfectly happy. But no system of morality, if left to itself, can compass this grandest and best of all consummations. What is morality? What does it say? What can it do? It says much; it can do little. Morality is, Do this, and thou wilt do right; Do this, and thou shalt prosper. But we need more than precept, or even more than promise, as a motive to morality. Power is necessary. Duty is hard, and we are weak; and temptations to evil are ever present and ever powerful. Here morality does not even profess to come to our aid. It does not hesitate to proclaim its impotency with no uncertain voice: "The good that I would, I do not; but the evil which I would not, that I do." "Meliora probo, deteriora sequor." It still utters the old cry of the heart's despair, "O wretched man that I am, who shall deliver me?" Morality, however well-meaning and well-judging, is, as a matter of fact, weak and unable to carry out its intentions. It is wish and desire, but little more; it is not fulfilment. What would man not be, did his good works but answer to a tithe of his good intentions or even of his well-meant attempts?

But morality comes short in another respect also. It fails to influence effectually the will. Man needs motives to well-doing; morality provides none. Why should I lead this hard life which men call virtue? What is in a name? Why not live a life of self-gratification, even though it should not go by the name of virtue? Why should Cato live when virtue itself is dead? What are thy motives, O Morality! to righteousness? Morality is silent: it is not perhaps absolutely dumb, but it speaks with a low and faltering voice.

There is also a further particular in which morality is defective. Morality does not carry us beyond this world, or even look beyond it. Morality does not, either in the Old Testament or in Greek or Roman philosophy, recognize a future state of existence. Its sphere is purely earthly and human. "Let us eat and drink to-day, for to-morrow we die," is in this respect good morality. Morality ends where this world ends; but man does not end there. In fact, morality in point of duration leaves man just where he needs countenance and help most.

So morality as a system—of which goodness and happiness are professedly the aim and end—is incomplete, most miserably so. It has a "form of godliness, but denying the power thereof." Still it is a form, and an indispensable form, and an eternal form, and least of all an empty form. It is the foundation and starting-point and eternal model of all our goodness. But it does not in itself contain means to that end. If man is to be good, it is clear that he must, while accepting morals as a law and as a perfect type, find elsewhere the means of filling in this form and fulfilling this law. Whither shall he turn? To what shall he look?

LI.—RELIGION THE COMPLEMENT OF MORALS AND THE FULFILLER OF THE LAW.

Morality is an empty form, beautiful and perfect, but still empty; religion fills it up. Religion is practically the complement of morals. Morality, as we have seen, is, as a complete goodness, in many essential respects found wanting. It is good as far as it goes, and points out the way still further than it goes; but it falls short practically of its high destiny. What morality lacks, Christianity supplies.

One grand defect, if not the greatest, of the moral scheme is, as we have seen, a lack of power; Christianity supplies this want. Christianity is power. It is a new birth, a new nature. Morality is human; Christianity is divine. It is a power *for us*. "Be strong in the Lord, and in the power of his might." Christ wrought miracles; so does the Christian. "Ye shall do greater things than these." Christ's religion, whatever else it may be or may not be, is certainly power for every conceivable moral or spiritual purpose—power to overcome evil, to work righteousness, to lay hold on eternal life. It professes at least to be all this; and this profession must needs be, in any inquiry we make as to what Christ's religion really is, a law to us, rather than the mixed sort of lives which so-called Christians are content to lead, or the views they carelessly hold. Well, if Christianity be indeed power, what a contrast here presents itself between the power of religion and the powerlessness of man's unassisted nature, or between grace and nature, or, which is the same thing, between the Law of Moses and Christ's Gospel!

Again, morality lacks incentives to well-doing; Christianity supplies them. In morals there is little but cold precept, a lukewarm sense of duty, to influence our will for good. But who can number the Christian motives to this end, or tell their force? What are they? Not merely a sense of duty, which is cold at best and needs rekindling on every fresh occasion, but love, peace, joy, gratitude, heaven. Motives there are everywhere, look where you will, present, past or future. God's gift of His Son is a motive in the past; the strength and comfort He affords His people day by day, are so many motives in the present; "such good things as pass man's understanding," and which are "prepared for them that love Him," are motives in the future.

Where will you find a motive of an honest and genuine character that is not pressed into the service of Christ's religion? Christianity is the highest enthusiasm, and enthusiasm is a motive-power. But Christianity is not enthusiasm only; it is the exact contrary as well; it is caution and calculation and prudence. You may "sit down and count the cost," as you are challenged to do, and you will find reasons why, after the very coolest computations, you should at all events hold fast your confidence. Art thou of what is called a sanguine temperament? There are motives for thee. Is thy nature cautious and circumspect? I do not say there are not even stronger motives for thee. So religion, in respect of motives to well-doing, is a new world, compared with that old world of mere law, of mere morality.

But not only does Christianity supplement morals in those several and important particulars in which we found morality to be wanting, but it enlarges indefinitely the sphere in which morality moves. It adds heaven to earth. Christianity, in its revelation of a new and eternal world, and of a God of love, and of the fact that "God so loved the world as to give His only-begotten Son," reveals new brotherhoods, new relationships, new affections, a new kingdom, a new life. Christianity, so far from being content with fulfilling the old morality or even elevating it, enlarges infinitely the boundaries within which it holds sway. By virtue of Christ's religion, morality enters into and takes possession of heaven itself.

Who can imagine the difference between the sphere of the old natural morality, as set forth either in the Old Testament or in the philosophy of Greece and Rome, and the sphere of the new Christian morality? The circle of the old morality is man and this world; the domain of the new morality is not only man, but God, and not only this world, but the world to come. Still it is not essentially a new morality. Aristotle and Plato are not out of date, except so far as to make perfect is to render out of date. The new morality, the Christian morality, is simply the old morality so made perfect and elevated and amplified that no further addition of a substantial character seems necessary or possible. It is the old morality, not destroyed, but made new, the "law fulfilled."

Hence practically Christianity and morality form one complete goodness. Morality without Christianity is imperfect and useless. Christianity without morality is impossible and unintelligible. It has neither a beginning nor middle nor end. "The kingdom of heaven is like unto leaven which a woman took and hid in three measures of meal until the whole was leavened." What would the "three measures of meal" be without "leaven"? They might be eatable, but they would not be palatable; they would not be bread. And what would leaven be without the "three measures of meal"? It would not even be eatable; it would be just what religion is without morality, nauseous and naught.

But is it really the case that religion just supplements morality? If so, can the coincidence, we are tempted to ask, be deemed accidental? If Christianity does indeed fill up, and just fill up, all that is wanting in human morals and in the matter of man's natural goodness, how do we account for this harmonious co-operation? Can it be accidental? Yes, if the sun in the firmament of heaven is accidental. Christ came to "fulfil the law"—that was not accidental. "Gratia non tollit sed perficit naturam," says Thomas Aquinas. Where two things, each of them of a complex and mysterious character, so accurately fit together as do man's natural morality and God's revelation, we are irresistibly led to the conclusion that the two things were originally intended for each other, and that the God of morals is also the God of the Bible.

Not that morals may not be regarded in some sort as a revelation as well as religion is, though not to the same extent. The Old Testament is a revelation of morality, of law, of natural law, of the law of man's nature; the New Testament is a revelation of what is necessary to make law perfect, to fulfil the law, that is of religion. Thus the relation between the Old Testament and the New Testament is in the main that which subsists between morals and religion.

LII.—RELIGION A USURPER IN GENERAL, PARTICULARLY IN THE SPHERE OF MORALS.

Religion—meaning thereby particularly, but in its spirit by no means exclusively, the Church of Rome—has been a usurper in politics, in astronomy, in geology—in short, in every department of human thought and action; but in no one sphere has it displayed its peculiar spirit of encroachment more than in the region of morals. Religion, in the domain of morals, is, properly speaking, a handmaid: she has reigned as queen. These Thoughts have wofully fallen short of their mark, if the necessity has not been impressed upon the reader of a thorough subordination, in thought and life, of religion to law in the widest sense—in other words, to reason and morality. Only in proportion to this subordination can the infinite confusions of religions and religious people ever be expected to come to an end.

LIII.—IMPORTANCE OF DETERMINING WHETHER OF THE TWO IS GREATER, RELIGION OR MORALITY.

It is not a mere speculation, but a problem of the highest practical importance, to determine whether religion or morality is to predominate; that is, whether, so far as they are connected—and they are most closely akin, woof and warp as it were—religion has jurisdiction over morals, or morals over religion. The Pope claims to be supreme in faith and morals—as though the domain of faith included, as a matter of course, that of morals. But does it? If faith is supreme, then all good Catholics, acknowledging as they do and must the Pope's jurisdiction in matters of faith, must also confess him to be supreme in the things of morality. But if morality is predominant and faith subordinate, then it is possible at any rate to conceive that we might, at one and the same time, deny the Pope's supremacy in morals, and allow it as regards faith.

It is a stroke of policy, to say the least, on the part of the Romanist Church, to regard morals as a subordinate branch of faith; for how can you call him to account for a breach of the sixth or eighth commandment, who has jurisdiction over the whole Decalogue? How, for example, are we ever to decide concerning the right or wrong of the massacre of St. Bartholomew, if religion is supreme over morals? On what religious principle is this deed to be tried? What are religious principles? To persecute to the death our neighbour, if he will not see with our eyes and speak with our voice? What are the religious principles common to Catholicism and Protestantism? Their mutual relation is that of protest.

But if we hold that morality is greater

than religion, and that the latter is bound to give way to the former where the two are not in agreement, then it would be at least possible to come to a conclusion as to the nature of the act and deed of St. Bartholomew's-eve. We are all of us at least tolerably well agreed as to what justice is; and truth and mercy and morality are the same essentially all the world over. We should have no difficulty in concluding, according to these moral principles, were but considerations of religion out of the way, whether the deed of that eve is to be applauded or execrated—whether it is to be set down to the debit or credit of the Church of Rome. If we find that it is not according to morality, then we continue our inquiries no further: we do not hesitate to conclude that much less is it to the credit of religion; for religion ought to be, if it is anything at all, a better morality, and not a worse—the fulfiller of the law, not its destroyer.

LIV.—MORAL SENSE AND EXPERIENCE THE TWO ARBITERS OF MORALS.

How do we determine truth in morals? By our moral sense, to begin with. We feel an action to be right or wrong, honourable or dishonourable, pure or impure; just as we perceive with our bodily eye this colour to be white, and that to be black, and that other colour to be neither white nor black, but a sort of gray; only the sense by which we make these moral distinctions is an inner sense—not the eye of the body, nor even of the intellect. But not by our moral sense only or conclusively are we able to distinguish between good and evil morally. Our senses are not infallible, and therefore not final. The moral sense may be dull—not to say blinded—or it may need a corrective, or it may not speak with exactly the same voice in all peoples or in all individuals. For example, the moral sense of Europe pronounces decidedly in favour of monogamy; the moral sense of the East is on the side of, or at least not against, a plurality of wives. Or as regards truth in word and justice in deed, who would affirm that man's moral sense speaks everywhere and always with the same voice?

In short, man's moral sense is not infallible. You may make too little of it, as you do if you deny its existence and authority altogether; but you may also make too much of it, as you do if you establish it as sole arbiter in the moral world. What, then, is to decide in case the moral sense is doubtful? The good or evil consequences that follow the action or course of life in question, must determine the character of that particular action or course of life. Experience is the interpreter in doubtful cases of morality, and the final court of appeal in all cases. The well-being of man, his happiness, his growth in whatsoever things are "pure and lovely and of good report," and, finally, his perfection, as it was the end of his creation, so it is also the end and test of his morality. By its fruits, in the long-run, our morality stands or falls.

So just as religion rests philosophically upon faith, or the religious sense, and experience, so also morality rests upon the two-fold basis of moral sense and experience—the moral sense or senses furnishing the materials, and experience working up these materials, and drawing from them conclusions, which in their turn again serve as bases for further results. For science means progress. Where there is no progress—where we are continually gyrating in a circle, or not moving perhaps at all—we have as yet, we may be quite sure, failed (if, indeed, we have tried) to hit upon that essential of all essentials, the right method of procedure.

And not only do we, by means of this method of experience, make progress in objective moral truth, point after point being added to the gradually increasing stock of established truths; but the moral nature itself is, *pari passu*, invigorated and quickened. "The senses by reason of use are exercised to discern both good and evil" (Heb. v. 14). We go on and on,

"Till old experience doth attain
 To something like prophetic strain."

So whatever our moral sense may be to begin with—and it is not alike strong and lively in all—it becomes a sense of higher power and quality to go on with, and most of all to end with.

Why has ethical science (if, indeed, there be a science worthy the name) made such small progress, if any, since the days of the Stoics and Epicureans? Why is morality, so far as regards its scientific treatment, still hardly better than a "rudis indigestaque moles," "without form and void," as though chaos in this respect had never yet come to an end? Because this so-called science has been treated purely as a speculation, and not practically—not as a matter of the moral sense to begin with, and experience (or utility, if any one prefers to call it so) to make perfect with. Treat it practically as a science, and if there is truth in it—and there is—it will no longer stand still. It will begin to move, and it will move rapidly.

LV.—JUDAISM AND CHRISTIANITY—IN WHAT RELATION DO THEY STAND TO EACH OTHER?

Judaism and Christianity stand to each other in substantially the same relationship as morals and religion. Judaism is all law, and (broadly speaking) no gospel; Christianity is all gospel, and (again speaking generally) no law. Put the two together, first divesting them respectively of all non-essentials, and you have a complete religion, law and gospel; the law as a foundation, "a form of godliness," and the gospel rendering the law possible, and realizing it and making it perfect. But here arises the difficulty. Who or what shall determine in either case what is essential and what is superfluous? And what as to the grand problem of all, which of the two is in itself, we will not say the more important, but the end of all—law or gospel? Is the gospel the end of the law, or is the law the end of the gospel? We have laid down the principle that the law, or morality, is, philosophically speaking, supreme, and that the gospel is the means, and the only means, to that end. Is not this what our Lord himself affirms in so many words: "I am not come to destroy the law and the prophets, but to fulfil."

To this formal subordination of gospel to law—gospel being the means, and law being the end—we cannot suppose the Jew would in the abstract have any objection whatever; indeed, we should hardly be wrong in supposing that it would be the one inducement which, more than any other, would reconcile him to the union of gospel and law; but does the Christian see the case in the same satisfactory light? Does he not, as a matter of course, put gospel above law? Be this, however, as it may, this controversy as to the relative pre-eminence of law and gospel is the main point at issue—so much so, that no hope of the conversion of the Jew to Christianity is within the range of probability until this first and great question is out of the way.

This conversion of the Jew to Christ and his gospel is of course an indispensable condition of the amalgamation of Christian and Jew in one religion; but is there no need on the other side of a conversion of the Christian to that supremacy of law which is the fundamental principle of Judaism, if the two are ever to meet on common ground? You will never convert the Jew to Christianity, *as the Christian religion is*, with its absolute claims, especially in the matter of the pre-eminence of gospel over law. Nor, on the other hand, will you ever reconcile Christianity to Judaism, *as the Jewish religion is*, with its law everywhere as a burden grievous to be borne, and its gospel nowhere to render possible, not to say acceptable, this intolerable yoke.

We do not, therefore, expect to harmonize Christianity *as it is* with Judaism *as it is*. What we can do is to endeavour to discover the true relation of law and gospel, and how far they have deviated, the one and the other, from the right path, and occupied each other's ground. When we have made clear this fundamental relationship, there is nothing to prevent us, in the first instance, doing homage to this ascertained truth ourselves; and, that done, it would not be presumption on our part if we approached the Jew and besought him to make the same obeisance, and likewise to submit, not to us or to our religion, but to what is simply religious truth. Will he do so? It is at least possible, despite the prejudices, and not without reason, on his part of 1800 years. This great principle being confessed on both sides, Jew and Christian will then be one; the middle wall of partition will be really and for ever thrown down; then will there be one Lord, one faith, one religion.

Christian science may or may not be a possibility, so that religion shall rest, not merely on a basis of faith, but upon experience as well; nevertheless, all depends upon this possibility. Make religion knowledge, and not a mere arena of conflicting beliefs, and there ought to be no insuperable difficulty between Jew and Christian. Give the law its rightful place, and it is possible law and gospel may come to terms. Allow that to be "perfect as our Father which is in heaven is perfect" is the end of man and of all religion, and perhaps the Jew may come to see that the only means of compassing this end is "the gospel of our Lord and Saviour, Jesus Christ." Make sure of the Christian first of all, as we have it in our power to do if we will, and all further difficulties as to the Jew may be expected in due time to vanish. But supposing Christianity to remain as it is, with faith as its sole foundation, and faith upon faith as its superstructure (the last and great effort of faith being a belief in human infallibility), and law and experience nowhere, you may then with equal certainty predict that Judaism will remain as it is.

A science of religion, and not a mere following of our natural religious instincts, is absolutely called for, if Jew and Christian are ever to become one on any solid and permanent basis. Science is truth, and truth is neither barren nor unfruitful; and one principal fruit of a science of religion would be a substantial unity as regards Jew and Christian. The mistake intellectually of the Jew is, that he undervalues, if not ignores, the gospel; the corresponding error of the Christian is, that he underrates the law. The consequence is, that religion is to the Jew an intolerable burden, and to the Christian not so exclusively a "glorious liberty" as not to degenerate at will into arbitrariness and dissoluteness. The Jew is right, so far as he vindicates law and values it as the "pearl of great price," and "loves not his soul unto the death," in comparison of those "oracles of God" that have been committed to his trust. The Christian is in the right, so far as he upholds the gospel and glories in the "liberty wherewith Christ has made him free," and is resolved not to be "entangled again with the yoke of bondage," and maintains earnestly that law without gospel is a dead and impossible thing.

Only put these two together, law and gospel, in just measure and in their rightful places, and you have a complete religion, no part lacking: you have Old Testament and New Testament inseparably one, neither Judaism nor Christianity exclusively, but the two so wedded together that it is impossible without deadly violence to put them asunder. Let Jew and Christian each for himself seek and find the truth (and not be content with one exaggerated and diseased side of it, as at present), and the antagonism of 1800 years will cease, never to be renewed. On the foundation of faith only, or law only, Jew or Christian will never realize the blessing of unity or any other blessing; on the basis of faith, made Christian science, if such a thing is possible, they undoubtedly may, and certainly will, become religiously one. Christian science may be impossible, as you, my reader, are perhaps thinking; but if so, there are hosts of glorious expectations that are vanity too.

LVI.—JUDAISM AND CHRISTIANITY IN MATTER ONE, IN FORM DIVERSE.

Religion may be viewed under two aspects, matter and form. As regards the material, whereof the Jewish and Christian forms of faith consist, this material is altogether Jewish, no less in Christianity than in Judaism itself. The materials of the Christian religion the Christian is entirely indebted to the Jew for; he has simply appropriated them and dealt with them according to his good will and pleasure, with or without giving of thanks. Could there indeed be a more striking instance of thanklessness than has been shown in Christianity towards the Jew, in return for the benefits the Jew has conferred upon him in the matter of his religion? What did Moses and the Prophets and the Psalms deserve in the way of thanks? What acknowledgment have they received?

So much as to materials. But the question as to form is not so simple. How have these materials respectively been worked up by the Jew on the one hand, and the Christian on the other? Have Jew and Christian shaped their course on the same lines, so as to produce on the whole the same form? Not in the least. They have worked up religion, each of them, into a form peculiar to its respective framers; and these forms are not only not identical or even sympathetic, but they are more or less antagonistic. The Jew has found only, or mostly, law in these materials, and has worked them up mainly into a system of law; the Christian, on the other hand, has seen nothing but gospel in these same materials, or what might be interpreted as gospel or turned to a gospel purpose, and so has produced what is mainly, if not absolutely, a gospel. So out of these same original materials of Old Testament and New Testament, which are all of them in their nature and origin purely Jewish, have resulted two, not agreeing, but opposing, systems of religion, the one essentially law, the other essentially gospel.

How comes it to pass that, the materials in the two cases being the same, the resulting forms should be so unlike each other? Consider the natures of the Jew and Christian respectively, and then perhaps you will understand how, out of these same materials, when worked up by natures so different, forms so unlike, even amounting to antagonism, should be evolved; for it is not the material chiefly that constitutes likeness or unlikeness, but the spirit that is breathed into that material, which in the present case is a Jewish spirit on the one hand, and a Gentile spirit on the other. The Jew took this chaos of religious material and conformed it substantially to his own image and likeness; the Christian took it and made it in the same way essentially a reflex of his own nature. The Jew made of it a law like himself; the Christian fashioned it into a gospel like unto himself. Religion is said to convert us, and so it does; but do not we also, by way of reaction, convert religion to ourselves? St. Paul was converted to Christianity; but did not the Apostle also in a measure convert Christianity to himself? Is Christ's religion what it would have been outwardly and formally if Saul the persecutor had never become Paul the Apostle? Would it not have been in form infinitely more like Judaism than it is? And suppose the Jews as a people ever to be converted to Christianity (understanding by Christianity the present Church forms), would this conversion leave the religion to which they were converted as it was before, only with an increase of numbers? Would not this accession of what are now heterogeneous elements in some ways modify Christianity? Action and reaction are in religion, as in mechanics, equal and opposite. In religion it is seen more clearly than elsewhere what manner of men we are. No wonder, then, that the same materials, in such different hands as Jew and Gentile, should work up into forms so dissimilar as Judaism and Christianity.

LVII.—IS GOD ANGRY WITH US WHEN WE ARE WHAT IS TERMED CRITICAL IN RELIGION?

Is God angry with us when we doubt whether the things we believe in really are so—when we act on the principle, not of doubting, be it observed, what God says, but of questioning whether the Word imputed to Him is really His Word, or only the word of men as men? Or if it is indeed His Word, it may be we doubt whether the meaning usually put upon it is the right meaning. Does such a spirit of criticism evince an unbelieving state of mind, or disinclination to accept God's revelation to man, and a wish to find excuses? We cannot think so. Not only is such an inquiring state of mind commendable in itself, as betokening a love of truth, but it cannot but be regarded as well-pleasing in the sight of God.

Was God angry with Galileo? The Pope was, and his Council; but was He who is the Pope's Pope? And is not truth in religion the same thing as truth in astronomy, only infinitely more important? Are not the blessings of truth much more precious in religion, and the consequences of error much more disastrous? So far from God being displeased with us when we inquire concerning the things of religion whether they are really what they appear to be, this is precisely the work which, in religion more than in any other thing, God has given *our minds* to do. Remember it is written, "Thou shalt love the Lord thy God," not only "with all thy heart," but "with all *thy mind.*"

LVIII.—RELIGION, AS TO THESE THOUGHTS, AN INDIVIDUAL CONCERN ONLY.

A Christian may be regarded as to his religion from a two-fold point of view. In the first place, he may be considered simply as an individuality—as having, that is, no necessary connection with his fellow-christian—as receiving nothing from him, and owing nothing to him, but subject to himself alone, to his own conscience, and his own judgment—as being, in a word, thoroughly isolated and independent in thought, feeling and action. But at the same time he is not merely an individual, and as such independent of his fellows, but he is a member of the Christian community as a whole, and therefore in this sense not his own master, but under authority of some kind—subject not to his own judgment and conscience only, but to the universal judgment of all those who, with himself are professed disciples of the same Lord and Master.

It is solely in the former of these characters that these Thoughts regard the Christian, that is as an individual, not as a member. We are Alexander Selkirk in his island of Juan Fernandez. We have nothing whatever to do, in respect of these Thoughts, with the Church as a whole: otherwise we should be under a necessity of making the inquiry, What is the Church? Is it the Church of Rome, where membership is everything and individuality nothing? Or is it the Church of England, where the Church is something and the individual Churchman something, but it is not easy to say in what relation these two stand to each other, or what they amount to when put together? Or is it some one or other of the so-called Nonconformist or Congregational churches, where, speaking broadly, individuality is everything and the church nothing?

We might argue, were it necessary, that the state of things in the present day in the Christian world is such that believers might be thought to be practically absolved from all church obedience or allegiance, and to be free to act independently of whatever goes under the name of Church. Certainly there never was a time when Christians individually—if they are men of thought, and bring their thoughts to bear upon their religion—were thrown so entirely back upon themselves.

But we will not argue here on the ground of the present state of contradictions and confusions in the Church, or upon the indefinableness of the word Church. We do not need to do so. We may take the Church at its best and purest possible, not in its present wretched condition of schisms and disruptions, of hatreds and strifes, but in its most glorious unity conceivable—such a unity as it has never yet been its lot to enjoy, but which will one day constitute its glory, if it be, as it professes to be and as we believe it to be, the truth. What is the Church at best, and what could it do for us at most, as regards the particular case of our present inquiry concerning Christian knowledge? Can it impart to us a knowledge of the truth of Christianity, such a knowledge as we are in these Thoughts in pursuit of?

Suppose the Church even to be infallible, which is the utmost that can be conceived concerning it, what could even this infallible Church do for us in the way of Christian evidences? Can it give us knowledge over and above faith? Do you say it can, and then we are perfectly safe? Pardon me, my good friend; what we really rest upon in such a case is, not the infallibility of the Church, but *our belief* in that infallibility—a distinction which makes all the difference in the world. Infallibility (if, indeed, human infallibility is not an absolute contradiction in terms, just as we might speak of a round square or a four-sided circle) may be a good and sufficient foundation to rest upon; but what sort of a foundation is our belief in that infallibility? What is our belief worth? What are we worth? Are we infallible—we, with our ignorance and prejudice—we, with our blindness and selfishness?

Let a man only reflect, and he will soon come to the conclusion that to rely upon an infallible Church, as the single-minded Romanist fondly imagines he does, or upon an infallible Scripture, as is the kindred belief of Protestantism, is to rest simply upon self—that is to say, upon *our belief* that the Church or the Scripture, as the case may be, is infallible. In plain terms, whatever the Church may be in itself, or the Bible in itself, we occupy simply the place of believers; and what we in reality rest upon is, not that infallible authority, as we might even honestly suppose, but our belief in that infallibility.

So it is impossible for us, on the foundation of Church, however high the Church may stand in our estimation or really be in itself, to get beyond faith. The Church can never put us in a position to say, I *know* that Christ died for my sins, and rose again for my justification. Not even an infallible Church could do this for us; so that even to hold the Church to be infallible makes just no difference at all to us as regards the purport of these Thoughts. We had faith before, and it may be a sufficiency of faith; and we have no more than faith now, and never can have more, on the basis of Church or Bible as foundation. If a man, instead of comforting himself with the persuasion that he relies upon the Church or the Bible, would only reflect that what really gives him comfort is his belief in the Church or the

Bible, and would then try to estimate accurately what he himself is, as a foundation, and not what Church or Bible is, or what he supposes them to be, he would appraise more justly his true position. His high-sounding Church or Bible infallibility would soon come down to the level of his miserable and prejudiced self.

Besides, we must not forget that if our belief in the infallibility of the Church or of the Bible makes the Church or the Bible true, the unbelief of that unbeliever, whoever he may be, equally makes the Church or the Bible to be false. My belief one way is worth just as much as his unbelief the other way, and no more. But neither belief nor unbelief counts as one jot in the way of evidence in one direction or the other. In short, the Church or the Bible, as the case may be, provides us simply with matter of belief: the Bible or the Church speaks, we believe or we do not believe, and there the matter ends, so far as our relation to Bible or Church is concerned. We believe what the Bible or the Church says, and there we stop: we can get no further under the guidance of either.

If we would have more, we must find that greater and more precious treasure for ourselves. We must set out for this purpose on a solitary journey, and traverse a hitherto unexplored country. This work of Christian evidence is not a matter of books or study, nor can it be done by proxy. If accomplished at all, it must be undertaken and carried out by the individual on his sole and undivided responsibility. The Christian is, and ever must be, in his "heart of heart," a lonely man, unless he is content to be to the end of life's chapter one of the many, with faith it may be, and indeed a superabundance of it, but without experience, and therefore without, in the full sense of the word, religion.

LIX.—NOTWITHSTANDING ANY KNOWLEDGE WE MAY ACQUIRE, WE WALK BY FAITH, NOT BY SIGHT, TO THE END.

Well, and suppose this pilgrimage over, and successfully so—what then? Is faith at an end? Is faith now superseded? As touching particular individuals, undoubtedly, in certain respects. What was doubt is now satisfaction. What was anxiety is now peace of mind. When we come to know what hitherto we have only believed, however firmly, we naturally rest upon that confirmation in gladness and serenity of spirit. Blind Bartimæus, when Christ has opened his eyes, no longer *believes* merely that the Saviour can and will do this great thing for him: it is done, and he knows it. The doubt of the past is merged in the certainty of the present, and faith is lost in knowledge. The light of the risen sun puts out the stars. Faith vanishes in such cases, or rather it hardens and crystallizes into firm conviction. When we know a thing, we no longer concern ourselves about reasons for believing it. Knowledge, so far as we have it, must supersede faith to the same extent. How far that knowledge may reach altogether is a matter which experience alone can determine. Never, however, can faith become knowledge in so great a measure as to make religion knowledge to us rather than faith; for "we walk by faith, not by sight," not only to begin our Christian course with, but to end life with altogether.

LX.—OUR KNOWLEDGE INCOMMUNICABLE AS KNOWLEDGE.

Never does our religious knowledge, whatever it may amount to, go beyond ourselves as knowledge. It began with us, and it ends with us. In the form of knowledge it is incommunicable. We impart what we have found—and what is the worth of this communication to our listener? It is a confirmation of his faith—nothing more.

And yet it is of some value even so, as faith, though not as knowledge. Just as it is natural that a believer should go on from faith to knowledge, and indeed necessary, where his faith is a living faith,—so it is equally to be expected that he should not keep silence as to what he has found in the course of his journey from this world to the next.

All this is so much a matter of course, and so entirely what we should look for, that we should feel no slight disappointment were we never to meet with such recorded experiences. A doubt, moreover, might even trouble our minds as to the reality of religion altogether, were we never to find those corroborations of our beliefs which we felt we had a right to calculate upon in the experience of others. We are now satisfied: we find just the sort of evidence we were looking for, on the supposition of the reality of faith. And not only as dispellers of doubts may such experiences be regarded when made public, but as aids to faith. They do not, it is true, turn our faith into knowledge—that is not to be anticipated; but they do support and strengthen our faith.

Whatever of edification or utility there be in works on theology in the ordinary sense—such as there is no lack of in the present day—there is at least a shorter, if not more satisfactory, way of imparting religious truth to others, and that is simply to set down what you yourself have found, if anything, of truth in your journeying heavenward by faith. A few grains of such experience, simple, pure and genuine, are worth many a bushel of what is called divinity. What we stand in need of in the matter of religious evidence is not divinity, but humanity; not the clouds, but terra-firma. Otherwise what are we doing but building our eternal home, not even on the sand, but in the air? The song of good old Simeon, that "sweetest of all canticles," to use Lord

Bacon's words, is what we require in the way of divinity or theology: "Lord, now lettest thou thy servant depart in peace, for mine eyes have seen thy salvation." This is not faith in God merely, such as had been Simeon's all the days of his life—it is faith in its ripeness and perfection—it is knowledge of God, the "end of our faith, even the salvation of our souls."

LXI.—IS IT POSSIBLE TO DRAW THE LINE BETWEEN THE CHRISTIAN IN HIS INDIVIDUALITY AND IN HIS RELATION TO CHRISTIANITY AS A WHOLE?

Though religion as to these Thoughts is an individual concern only, we cannot, nevertheless, altogether lose sight of the fact that each individual is a member also of the whole Christian community, as well as an individual Christian. On both this individuality on the one hand, and this membership on the other, great, if not equal, stress is laid in the New Testament. The believer is free and independent. "If the Son shall make you free, ye shall be free indeed," says the Saviour (John viii. 36); and St. Paul speaks of "the glorious liberty of the children of God" (Rom. viii. 21). But we need be at no pains to multiply passages. Such is the general tenor of the New-Testament teaching as to the Christian in his individuality. He is "free indeed." He is not, unless he voluntarily descends from that high station which is his birthright, the "servant of men." Even a St. Paul does not claim "dominion over his faith."

But he is not merely regarded as an individual, and therefore independent; he is at the same time a member of the Christian community as a whole, and therefore in this sense not his own master. On this side of the Christian character also Scripture lays great stress. We are "members one of another." "Ye are the body of Christ, and members in particular." "No man liveth to himself, and no man dieth to himself."

Such are the sayings of St. Paul; and the words of our Saviour to the same effect had already gone before. "I am the vine; ye are the branches." "If two of you shall agree on earth as touching anything that they shall ask, it shall be done for them of my Father which is in heaven. For where two or three are gathered together in my name, there am I in the midst of them" (Matt. xviii. 19, 20). "I pray that they may be one, even as we are one" (John xvii. 22).

So Scripture, while it represents the Christian as individually and gloriously free, puts him also before us as at one with, and living on terms of the closest fellowship with, his fellow-christians, and so in the enjoyment of fuller and richer blessings than would otherwise be his portion. But where is the line to be drawn? In what respect is the Christian free, and how far is he bound? How far is he to assert that freedom which is his purchased possession; and how far is he to be ready to surrender it for the good of the Church at large, and indirectly for his own greater benefit? This is a practical problem not easy to solve. Perhaps there is no such hard-and-fast line, as would unquestionably be highly convenient if we could only find it. Assuredly there is not such a line drawn as regards the kingdoms and other communities in general of this world, where the same problem is continually awaiting solution.

How much liberty is it good and right politically for a man to reserve for himself; and how much is it fair and reasonable he should surrender to the government of his country, be that form of government what it may? The line is drawn differently in different nations and peoples, and is continually shifting, and certainly does not seem to be approaching fixity. How variable in quantity and quality is individual liberty in Russia, in Germany, in England, in the United States of America; and therefore how varying also, only inversely, the power of the central authority! Well, can the problem present itself otherwise in the sphere of religion? Perhaps not; we have extremes here and variations here, and no universally agreed-upon line of demarcation between what is the right of the individual Christian, and what is due to the Church of which he professes to be a member.

There is the Church of Rome, as one extreme, claiming and receiving the full surrender of the individuality of its members— their individual conscience, their individual judgment. On condition of this absolute self-sacrifice, Rome undertakes to make us safe for eternity; as though man could receive back aught worthy the name of salvation, when his liberty, his conscience, his common sense, his manhood, are all gone. What, we may well ask, is left to such a man worth saving? At the other extreme we have in this country what is called Dissent or Nonconformity. Here individuality may be said to reign supreme, the surrender that is made to Church being merely nominal; so much so, that it would almost seem to be more outspoken in these communities to abandon the idea of Church altogether, the word Church meaning in their case not so much the subordination of self to Church as of Church to self.

Neither of these extremes can reasonably please us. It cannot be required of a Christian man that he should be a slave in his religion, neither can it be lawful for him so to eschew unity in his religion as to sacrifice entirely unity to his own individuality. Where lies the mean between these two extremes? Is it the Church of England? We will not argue the point. Whatever the line may be, its indispensable conditions would seem to be *both* a real freedom on the one hand, and a real subjection and submissiveness on the other. These conditions being satisfied, perhaps it is allowable that we draw the line where we judge best, if we can only find one. It may be that the same line would not serve equally well in all cases and under all circumstances.

This much, however, does appear practically to follow from the fact of our bearing this two-fold character of individuality and membership, that whatever we undertake, which we may regard as of importance, of a religious nature, in our individual capacity, we should first ask ourselves seriously, before we take the matter in hand, whether we are at liberty to act as an independent individuality in this particular, or, as members of Christianity as a whole, are bound to take some other course, or, it may be, to refrain from acting altogether.

LXII.—BY WHAT RIGHT HAVE WE TAKEN IN HAND THESE THOUGHTS?

By what right have we presumed to take in hand and to resolve the great problem which has been engaging our attention in these Thoughts? How may I know that Christianity is true? I do believe, but I am not content with believing; how may I *know?* This inquiry concerning our rights might, we confess, seem to have been more in place when we began, than now when our task is as good as accomplished. It is nevertheless one with which we should not then have been able to deal so effectually as we may be supposed to have the means of doing now. Whatever the right may be, we have at least shown that we have not lacked the power to take in hand this problem and bring it to what we may consider to be a satisfactory conclusion. This is the chief thing; for what is the use of a right where there is not the power to enforce the right? We have at all events done what we proposed to do, and to our no small contentment.

Nor have we met with any such obstacle on our way as was of a nature to arouse the suspicion that we were engaged on some unlawful enterprize. Difficulties we have experienced, and no light ones; but we have encountered no such hindrances as would seem to suggest that we were on forbidden ground, or employed in some vain or unwarrantable undertaking. On the contrary, what we have found by the way, apart from what we expected to discover as the final result of our explorations, has fully repaid us for the toils and anxieties of the enterprize itself. What, indeed, have we been doing but simply that which it was our bounden duty to do? What is a man's duty, if it be not to inquire after truth, and to "search for her as for hid treasures"? What is this but religion in its very essence, no less than the highest morality? So we have no misgiving as to our right in this matter. Whatever is a man's duty is at all events his right—is a pursuit in which he is justified in setting at nought all interference, whether from his own easy-going self or from them that are without.

So far therefore as our individuality is concerned, we can have no qualms whatever respecting the perfect propriety of our proceedings as touching the matter of these Thoughts. But we are not individuals merely—individuals and nothing more ; we stand in a certain relation to universal Christendom ; we are members of the Church Catholic, that is of the "company of all faithful people." Hence a consideration arises as to what becomes of our individual rights when put face to face with the obligations of our Christian membership— when we regard ourselves, not as absolute units, but as units in relation to the myriads of equally significant Christian units around us, to whom our problem, if it is anything, is just as significant as it is to us, and who may all of them be supposed to have just the same voice as we have in the matter in hand.

Is there not at least a call for hesitancy here? Not at all. We reply plainly that our natural rights, as regards our special problem, remain just where they were when we have taken fully into account Church rights. What can the whole of Christendom, however well inclined, do for us in this matter of Christian experience? Can the Church, by means of its catholicity, endue us with any knowledge of Christianity apart from and higher than faith? The Church is an embodiment of the Christian faith, and beyond that it does not attempt to go. It imparts to us the Christian doctrines simply to be believed and practised, and that is all. Nay, whatever knowledge the Church might put us in possession of, supposing it to have it, this knowledge could not reach us as knowledge, but only as faith.

If we would have the Christian religion in its highest possible degree, that is to say as knowledge, this highest attainable stage can only be ours as the result of our own individual efforts and experience. But not only is it the case that the Church cannot, as regards its power, rise so high as to impart to us what is in the proper sense of the word Christian knowledge, but it cannot in another sense, and that is with a due recognition of its professed and, we may say, unalterable principles as to science. Christian theology—what is it? It is not human science; rather it is in principle the exact antipodes of human science. Its pursuit is not knowledge. Faith is its sphere, and within this sphere it scrupulously, and we may say religiously, keeps. In its length and breadth, and from foundation to topstone, it has to do with faith, and faith alone, and with the conclusions to be deduced therefrom.

Theology could not, without first abandoning its principles, be our guide in the ways of knowledge, as a thing higher than faith. Nay, where you naturally expect faith to stop and to give place to knowledge, it foils our expectations; it puts itself or is put in the place of knowledge, and as faith asserts a pre-eminence over knowledge.

Faith as regards Church doctrine is supreme over knowledge and overpowers it. What is transubstantiation? Here faith says one thing and our eyes say another, and faith overwhelms and leads captive knowledge. The true Catholic *believes* that a transubstantiation has taken place, though all the while he *knows* that the substances remain just what they were, and so he subordinates his knowledge to his faith. So also as to that kindred doctrine, the doctrine of Papal infallibility. We all know that the Pope is not infallible—that he is liable to mistakes, great or small, continually; but as good Catholics we believe him to be what we know him not to be, and here again faith triumphs over knowledge.

If we, as Catholics, repudiate this infallibility as a monstrous thing, we are assuredly inconsistent Catholics, for we have already allowed the principle again and again, and to abandon it now as a principle would be to stultify our past lives and to sap the foundations of the Church itself. It is the principle intellectually on which the Church—we might say any Church—is built, however much or little it may be kept within bounds.

These two doctrines, in fact, represent the complete subjection of human freedom and human reason to Church authority; and the heads of the Church, in insisting upon them without one jot in the way of abatement or qualification, know perfectly well the rôle they are enacting; while those who oppose them on the ground that such beliefs are absurd, may be in the right as a matter of reason, but they are nevertheless inconsistent Catholics. It is, in fact, because these doctrines do violence to reason and common sense outwardly and unmistakably that they are so insisted upon; were they in themselves reasonable, they might be, and in all probability would be, left to take care of themselves. The relation in which faith stands to knowledge in these two doctrines, it holds in respect of theology in general, though of course not to such an extent as to shock the common sense of mankind.

These doctrines, however, are no exceptions to the general rule, but only the most striking examples of it. Who could have imagined that faith, divine faith, heavenly faith, could ever have become what we see it to be in transubstantiation and Papal infallibility? How careful ought we to be not to suffer even the best and holiest of things to go one jot or tittle beyond their legitimate bounds! "Virtue itself turns vice, being misapplied," we must ever remember. All human things, however good in themselves, are only good in a particular way and to a certain extent. But men forget this; only let them get hold of a good thing, and they never can make too much of it, as though it were absolutely and eternally good; consequently their good sooner or later turns to evil. It is against the evil that is in good things that we shall do well to be more especially on our guard. Things bad in themselves are at least in this respect good, that they cannot deceive us.

But are we not digressing? If it be the principle of theology that faith, when it speaks in the name of religion, is to be accounted greater than the most absolute knowledge when it speaks in any other name, it must necessarily follow that theology should regard science as in some sort an unnecessary—nay, as an unholy thing—as, in fact, an enemy rather than a friend. The Church *must* decry science, seeing that science is antagonistic to the system on which theology is built; and it does decry it. Its instincts are against it, its policy is against it, so are its acts and deeds. Whenever the question is asked — and it is a standing question in these days—whether there be in reality any opposition between Christianity and Science, we must take care that we understand what is meant by the question before we commit ourselves to a reply.

If by Christianity is to be understood the birth, crucifixion and death of Christ, and his ascent into heaven, and all the facts appertaining thereto, as set forth in the Four Gospels and in the Acts of the Apostles—if by Christianity is meant these and the like facts, when they were as yet unsystematized, we need not hesitate to reply that there is no opposition at all between them—that religion and science will, if only the perversity of man will allow them to do so, live harmoniously and contentedly together; in other words, we admit, indeed we think we have shown, that Christianity is capable of scientific treatment and amenable to scientific laws.

But if we are to understand by Christianity Christian facts and Christian doctrine, as already embodied in Christian theology and worked up into the already prevailing Christian system, then we are equally bound to say that Christianity in this sense is not capable of scientific treatment, and for the simple reason that it has already been enshrined in a system which is just the opposite of science and irreconcilable therewith. Concord there will be between science and Christianity, provided the so-called Christian facts are taken for what they are worth to begin with — that is, as beliefs and nothing more — and then reduced to a science, as they are capable of being; but there is every antagonism between a method of inquiring after truth (the scientific method) which insists upon knowledge and cannot be satisfied with less, and a method (the dogmatic method) which is abundantly content with faith, and which, so far from "following on to know" the things it professes to believe, resolutely stops short at faith, and rather scorns knowledge than assigns it its proper place in relation to truth.

The Church system always has been, and is, and must be, at war with science, covert or open; and men of science must be *as such* opposed, we do not say to religion, but to what are called the evidences of religion, where beliefs are quietly assumed to be facts, and where the immeasurable difference is not recognized between knowing a thing to be true and only believing it to be so. It is this Church system, already existing and firmly grounded, which is the great difficulty in the way of a science of religion.

The ground is not clear for a science of religion, in the true sense of the word. So long as this opposing power is in force, there is and must be war between the science of religion as already embodied in theology, and which is regarded as a divine science, and that other which we profess to be merely human science, and which does not rest upon faith alone, but on faith as confirmed by experience. This war between science and religion will one day come to an end. "Mercy" (as religion) "and truth" (as science) "will meet together," and, once meeting, will never part asunder more.

They will go hand-in-hand, and "shine brighter and brighter unto the perfect day."

Meanwhile our duty is clear. If theology, or divinity, or whatever its most appropriate title may be, cannot, will not, must not, assist in or even countenance our individual researches after Christian truth, in the only worthy sense of the word truth, theology must at least not be suffered to bar the way. If it does make the attempt, we quietly, as we are at liberty to do, pass by on one side. We must not permit ourselves to be troubled in mind or turned from our purpose by this far-reaching and over-reaching power; though in presence of it we are, humanly speaking, but as dust in the balance. Indeed, we have not permitted ourselves to be in any sense detrimentally influenced by this opposite principle.

The Church has no rights whatever as against the individual in the inquiry we have been instituting in these Thoughts. It is the Church and not we that are to blame if we break down any barriers that may be set up to stop our way. Christian knowledge, as the ripeness and perfection of faith, is a field of labour for our own individuality, and for that alone. Whatever rights the Church may have (and it has rights, rightly considered), it is not entitled to interpose between the conscience of the individual and any researches in the realm of Christian truth he may be minded to prosecute. To allow such a right on the part of the Church would be to leave no right to the individual worth retaining. When our conscience is silenced, and our freedom of thought and action in matters of religion gone, what have we left which as men we can care to keep? When we are once brought down to say that bread is not bread, or that humanity is infallibility, at the bidding of our spiritual superiors, what is there remaining of us in any sense that writes us down men?

We go gladly with the Church, so far as

it is our duty to do so, whether in its confessions of faith, or in its ordinances, or what not of that character, even to the furthest bound of its legitimate tether; but when the Church puts its veto upon our thoughts—when it forbids us to help ourselves, though it cannot itself assist us—when it sets bounds to our inquiries after truth—"Thus far shalt thou go, and no further," lest thou imperil what we hold dear—then, in place of obedience, we part company in these matters with the Church, and quietly go our own way.

Whatever love a man may have for his Church, he does not even love his Church as he ought if his love of truth is not greater; and when we lay down the principle that the Christian as an individual has his individual rights, and those of the most precious description, which he must not suffer even universal Christendom to supersede or impair—what are we but at least lovers of truth, and certainly not enemies of what is, in the true sense of the word, Church? Follow truth in thy religion, and thou wilt find both truth and religion; follow religion in thy so-called prosecution of truth, and thou wilt find neither one nor the other. All depends upon what we put first to take the lead.

LXIII.—A FORECAST, OR CHRISTIAN SCIENCE IN THE FUTURE.

Will Christianity as a science ever hold a place in the religious world? Will it ever be, what it is not in any degree now, an acknowledged science, with more or less of a professed following? What is the prospect when we scan the future, and penetrate as far as our dim and blurred vision will permit? It may not be useless to make this inquiry, though it is beyond the scope literally of these Thoughts, which are concerned solely with Christians as individuals, and not as any recognized or organized whole. Do you answer with the trite proverb, "Magna est veritas et prevalebit"? So be it; but will truth prevail if left to itself and to its own inherent goodness? Like most aphorisms, this proverb is but a half-truth, or a truth in sound rather than in substance. You mistake it if you fold your hands and sit still under the comfortable conviction that truth will do the work for you, and you have simply to reap the harvest.

Truth has no power whatever if left to itself. We may, if we please, take for granted the truth of the principles we are advocating; it does not, however, follow that we are justified in taking for granted their ultimate triumph also, if discountenanced and unaided. Truth is indeed a weapon, and no light one; but where is the hand to wield it, and to strike blow upon blow? How many truths are there which have not even seen the light, which lie hid in the treasure-houses of earth and heaven, or are buried in the womb of time? Why have they not yet come forth, if truth unassisted is all-sufficient? How is it that truths live and flourish at one time and place, and wither or die at another, if truth is, so to say, unconditioned? How is it that truths ever fail or perish, if truth contains in itself all the indispensable elements of an inherent vitality?

So truth is not self-sufficient. Its success is conditional, not absolute. And what are the conditions? For one thing, truth is a seed, and seed implies a sower; as it is written, "A sower went out to sow his seed." Now what kind of sower must he be who would disseminate living truth, moral and religious truth, such as has for its own end the well-being and perfection of man; or, to drop metaphor, what qualifications are indispensable to him who would undertake and effectually carry out the task of implanting and propagating moral and religious truth? He has to begin with, of course, the truth in him which he professes to engraft and inoculate. Or rather, perhaps, we ought to say the truth has him.

There is a wide difference between our having the truth and the truth having us. What we have hold of, we may let go; what has hold of us, if it be truth, will not let us go. A man may be in many respects a man of truth, and yet may go no further in the way of truth than may seem good to him. For some reason or other he may stop short at the critical point, that point being where his interests and the interests of truth are no longer one. To such a one, truth is not a lord (the only relation in which truth, real truth, will ever consent to stand to us), but a menial. He does not live to it; he has no thought of sacrificing himself on its high altar. Not so the true disciple of truth: with him, truth is the first thing and the only thing; he does not regard truth as the mere abettor of his purposes; indeed, it is altogether out of his power to do so, for the truth has him, mind and heart, and he must follow it whithersoever it goeth. Is his labour in vain? No; every man has his reward in due season of one kind or another, and so has he. He who is thus emptied of self becomes a depository of truth, and that not of a useless or incommunicable sort as regards his fellow-men. So the truth is sown broadcast and spreads.

Not that we are to suppose that the power to impart truth follows as a matter of course from the possession of it. To picture a landscape in our minds and to put it on canvas are widely distinct things, and the former is very far from implying the latter. Just so of spiritual truth. Whatever truths of this character may be generated in our minds, it does not follow that we shall possess the power of realizing an adequate presentment of them in speech or writing. So to express ourselves as to make the hearer hear the truth and the beholder to see it, is a faculty very different from the power of discovering the truth or ourselves seeing it. An apostle of the truth, to do the work of an apostle, must be specially endued, not only with the truth, but with the word or expression of truth. St. Paul was right well aware of this principle when he says concerning his own teaching (1 Cor. ii. 13), "Which things we speak not in the words which man's own wisdom teacheth, but which the Holy Ghost teacheth."

So much as to the men, if truth is to take root and spread. It now remains only to inquire where is the ground, and ground of the right character; for a certain soil or preparation of the soil is necessary if the seed sown is not to be cast into the ground in vain. What is this indispensable condition or preparation of the soil? To speak plainly, and apart from figure of speech, can it be any other than what is commonly called a sense of sin, which sense of sin has for its precursor a sense of misery, an intolerable sense of misery? Misery is the seed-bed of truth. Were there no misery in the world, no progress would be possible in moral and religious truth. In moments of gloom, it may be, we are tempted to ask why this world was ever created at all, with misery permeating its inmost nature and stamped upon every feature, if not misery absolutely overpowering happiness. One thing, however, we need not be at any loss to comprehend, and that is, why it should be a world of misery if ever it was to be a world of truth in things spiritual. There may, indeed, be misery and no truth, for misery does not in itself generate truth; but never can the latter be where the former is not.

When men are happy, they are more or less contented, and loth to jeopardize their present lot by any agitation for a change; and even though we do succeed for a time in arousing them to the thought of better things, no sooner is the pressure relaxed than they revert forthwith to their original easy-minded condition. Why is the gospel said to be preached to the poor, as though there were no others in the world to preach it to? Because the poor are as a class the miserable; because, consequently, the minds of the poor are a congenial soil and in a state of receptivity. Put your higher moral and religious teachings, as worthy of all acceptation, before the rich, the happy, the prosperous, and the most eloquent words are to no purpose; they are "deaf to the voice of the charmer." First make these flourishing sons of earth as ill-to-do as they were before well-to-do, then the spell is broken, the scene changes, and they are now all devotion where they had not before "an ear to hear." Well may it be said, "Blessed are the poor"!

Thus there are two things which seem to be needful to the propagation of moral and religious truth, of what we may call living truth, truth in relation to man, as distinguished from truth relatively to the things of this material world; and these two things are, the right man and the right time. Truth, if left to itself, is nothing. It may or may not be beautiful to the spectator (all depends upon the eye), but it is of no account practically. It is helpless in the midst of foes. It is the sixth Henry at the head of Yorkist or Lancastrian forces, as the one or the other is for the time the stronger. It is not itself a king. The moment it presumes to lift up its puling voice, it is at once silenced, or, it may be, crushed at least temporarily out of account. It is at most in its solitary self "the voice of one crying in the wilderness," with no ear in the wilderness to hear. You may be a thousand times in the right ; but where are you if you have only ten thousand men to meet him that cometh against you with twenty thousand? When the devil disarms, then truth may. Be not content with the thought, "I have truth on my side," but muster your forces and beat up for fresh recruits. Be strong and of good courage, if you are to make any way.

Under what circumstances was Christianity itself first established? Under precisely those which upon inquiry we have found to be necessary to the life and final success of truth in these days. In the first place, there was a ripeness of time; and, secondly, not only the right time, but the right men. The time was, without doubt, propitious for a gospel of mercy and truth and justice, at that crisis of the world's history. Mankind was all wretchedness; sin and suffering were at their height. Cruelty and lust ruled the world. It was a world ready to perish, and it was conscious of its desperate state, and consequently prepared to receive a deliverer with open arms. No wonder there was throughout the Roman empire a wide expectation, perhaps born of necessity, that a Saviour was at hand.

Here, then, was the soil prepared to receive the good seed of joy and hope and love—the good seed of "the life that now is, and of that which is to come;" and with the time, behold the men, men of power and of the Holy Ghost, men who spake with tongues. What if Christ had not come when the time was ripe for his advent? What if he had not commissioned the Twelve? What if there had been no day of Pentecost? The world was in a perishing state; and if no Saviour had appeared in due time, "to put away sin by the sacrifice of himself," and to infuse a new life into the world, man would have been actually lost. Or if a Saviour, even this very Redeemer, had come, and the human race had been in a contented condition, the gospel would have fallen dead, no evangelization of the nations would have been attempted; or if the attempt had been made, and the gospel had been preached with divine power, "the Lord even confirming the word with signs following," it would have found but a listless reception from these happy and self-satisfied sons of earth.

How far may these two conditions, the time and the man, be thought to be now existent as the necessary conditions of a Christian science? They were present at the foundation of the gospel—how far can they be now thought to be forthcoming at what may be regarded as the topstone of the gospel? There is a sense, and an important one, in which the gospel was not given in the beginning. It was not revealed in any systematic or scientific sense. We shall not be surprised. The God of truth never presents truth completely, never bestows it under its scientific aspect. He furnishes man with what we may call the raw material, and leaves him to work up these materials scientifically as he will. Has God given man astronomy? He has given him the materials—sun, moon and stars, and all the host of heaven; but the science of astronomy is the work of man's own will and mind. He has never been told by the Creator that the sun stands still and the earth moves; nay, if he has been told anything, it is the contrary. He has after much labour found these things out for himself.

So in religion. The facts of religion are so many revelations from God, and God has given all that is indispensable in this respect—all needful heavenly facts, whether in heaven or brought down to earth from heaven. This hath God done; but it is man's part if he will—and if he will not, the work for ever remains undone—so to infuse an intellectual life into these materials as to bring them under the rule and sway of science. Christian science, therefore, when established, may be regarded as the complement of that gospel which was given eighteen centuries ago.

What shall we say then? Is it likely to be established now or soon? Can it in any sense be said to be in view when we scrutinize the future as far as mortal vision can reach? We will not venture to say that it is. The conditions of success are, we must confess, all but non-existent, so far as our earnest expectation can foresee. Where are the men? What kind of men are needed? What qualifications are indispensable in them? They must, of course, in the first place and above all, be men of religion, and that not merely of a nominal or superficial sort, but heart and soul and strength. In order that any one may determine scientifically whether Christianity is true, it is essential that he himself live the Christian life in its sincerity and in its all-sidedness. He must live the life of faith if he would put his faith to any test, so as to try it whether it is true or false.

So the scientific inquirer is to be a man of religion—that is abundantly clear—a man of religion in the best sense of the word. But not only a religious man is he to be, but a man of mind, and of a scientific cast of mind. This also follows as a matter of course. How can any other than a scientifically inclined man cultivate a religious science? If he is merely religious, he will be satisfied with believing; he will not care to "follow on to know the Lord" in the scientific sense of the words.

We see, therefore, that two distinct and, we may say, opposite qualifications are called for in him who would prosecute our method—a true faith and a sound reason harmoniously working together, and each in its own sphere; in other words, a strong common sense, and this sense brought to bear upon the things of religion. Such are the qualifications of the man who can really be said to be a follower of the science of religion. Can we then wonder that a science of religion has not only not as yet triumphed, but has hardly seemed to prefer a claim for recognition? How few are there who are possessed of the necessary two-fold endowment of heart and mind—the heart burning with zeal, and at the same time under the control of reason! Of scientific men pure and simple there is no lack; but they look slightingly for the most part on religion and religious people, religion being foreign from their thoughts; religious people also there are in the world, of almost every possible form and hue; but the very name of science, as applied to religion, is in the highest degree an astonishment to them.

How few, then, must there be who are at once scientific and religious—their science rationalizing their religion, and their religion sanctifying their science! Not many, certainly; especially if we take into account that it is not enough that the necessary qualities be present in a certain inert and somnolent fashion, but as the life and soul of the whole man. And what as to the time? Is the time ripe for a science of religion? Who wants it? Where is the cry of the discontented? Does it go up to heaven, or is it so much as heard upon earth? What is it at loudest but whispered in the ear in closets, or murmured in the secret places of the mind? The Christian world is content to be as it is in this respect. It *believes* that Christianity is true—what further assurance can it possibly stand in need of? Why should its self-satisfaction be disturbed? Why should it demand that a rigid canon of truth be applied to that of which there is already no doubt? To do that would be as much as to insinuate that there are searchings of heart as to the truth of religion; and in any case no good could possibly result.

So the Christian world for the most part is indifferent to a science of religion. How long is this indifference to continue? Not for ever. It is impossible it should so remain. The world does not stand still. See we nought in the future when we look well a-head? Yes; we foresee science constantly marching onwards, and annexing kingdom after kingdom of this world's knowledge under its benign but no less inexorable sway. Where will it stop? Not, we may be sure, until it has brought under its dominion every branch of human inquiry except religion. Will it arrest its course then? We cannot think so. A pressure will, in consequence of these continual successes on the part of science, have been indirectly brought to bear upon religion, which it will be found impossible to resist any longer—which, indeed, in the minds of those who have Christianity really at heart, there will be now at length no disposition to resist.

How will then stand the case between science and religion? Human science is the highest form of truth. Earthly knowledge, in all its departments, will have received the imprimatur of this highest form. But not so religion. It will not yet be held to be truth, in the sense in which earthly knowledge of all kinds proves itself to be so. Is religion to remain for ever in that state of comparative inferiority and consequent degradation? Is the taunt never to cease, but rather to grow continually stronger, that whereas human science *knows*, this divine science of religion only *believes*? Great and increasingly so will be the pressure of science upon religion as time goes on; until at length this indirect force will become irresistible, and then "the fulness of time" is come, the ground is ready for the seed; and the time, as it has never yet failed to do, will produce the men.

And now the gospel is complete. The believer is now able to render perfect obedience to that first and great commandment, "Thou shalt love the Lord thy God with all thy heart and soul and *mind*." Hitherto he has loved God, it may be, with his heart and soul, but assuredly not with his mind. However little the principles of science may be to the liking of the religious world, the time will come when they will force their way in spite of all likes and dislikes. Necessity, which has no laws, has no tastes either.

LXIV.—CONCLUSION, WHEREIN THE WRITER BIDS ADIEU TO THE READER AND LEAVES HIM HIS WORK TO DO.

These Thoughts being ended, what remains but that the writer of them should bid adieu to the reader? As to the practical conclusion, it is with the reader himself. Are these Thoughts true? Do they bear the stamp and impress of truth? Have they at least the countenance of the dictum of Descartes, "Les choses que nous concevons fort clairement et fort distinctement sont toutes vraies"? Are they of any practical value? If so, fail not to turn them to practical purpose. We have put before the reader a certain *method*, which he is to follow if he would know, and not merely believe, as men generally are content to do, that Christianity is true. The method is such as of itself to commend itself—and apart from its scientific bearings—to the religious man. Even supposing that from the scientific point of view the pursuit comes to nothing, he is only where he was; he has not wasted his time or lost his labour in a religious sense, inasmuch as the scientific and religious cultivation of Christianity are in the same direction, only with this difference, that it is the province of science to observe and judge, and of religion to believe and do. The materials are the same, only the treatment is different. It is possible to be religious without being scientific; it is not possible to be scientific in religion without being religious. So the conclusion of these Thoughts rests with the reader, if they are to be of any practical value to him. We are the way; he is the traveller.

But perhaps the reader, seeing that we have said so many words to him, may also have a word to say to us before he can regard the book as closed. What have you, on your part, found? he may not unnaturally be inclined to ask. You commend to us a certain course; you have, we may be sure, for you seem to be an honest man, trodden this same path on your own behalf—what have you found? What does it lead to? A natural inquiry, no doubt, but savouring perhaps more of curiosity and want of reflection than of good judgment. It is, to say the least, premature. Not yet, at all events, am I, the writer of these Thoughts, in a position to satisfy my interrogator. He must at any rate wait awhile. Life with me is not yet ended, though the sands are fast running low. No man can tell what he finds until the end is come. It is the end alone that justifies the beginning. Can you stand with me on the brink of the grave? Can you accompany me to the world of spirits? Can you then hear my confessions and experiences? But what am I committing myself to? Even though I could impart to you my experiences of the realities of Christian truth, and assure you that they are verily and indeed truth, of what benefit would this communication be to you? Unless you are already a believer, and on far stronger grounds than those which my individual assurance could afford, my evidence would not suffice to make you the believer which you now are not. You might, and probably would, take me to be a deceiver. "If they hear not Moses and the prophets, neither will they be persuaded though one rose from the dead;" and most certainly if you have not heard already the Bible, with its prophets, apostles and teachers, you would never hear me. On the other hand, if you are already a believer, my evidence would add nothing of weight to the faith you already have. Do not therefore appeal to my experience as to what verdict our method pronounces when put to the test. The inquiry is undoubtedly a natural one—for what is more natural than curiosity, especially in the things of religion?—but it is one that either could not be responded to, or the answer would be of no service when forthcoming.

But has not this demand as to what the writer himself has found, been already in substance met, though indirectly, and without any attempt on his part to satisfy it? What is it these Thoughts undertake to do? They profess to discover the way to truth in the matter of religion. The pursuit has been an impartial one; at least we have done our endeavour to make it so. Has the result been favourable to the truth of Christianity, in the opinion of the writer? The very fact that these Thoughts are permitted to see the light, is a proof at least that he who publishes them abroad can conclude nothing to the contrary. Why should they have been made publicly known else? Would it not have been absurd to lay down carefully and painfully a road that leads to nothing? Who would not, the moment he finds his attempt vain, at once cut his labours short in such a case, and thank God that he has not at least gone further in what must ultimately have ended in nothing, however long he had persevered?

Suppose the result of these investigations had, if possible, been unfavourable to the religion we believe in; suppose we had found, to our thinking, that this method, while it was the true method, bore no fruits on the side of Christian truth, but rather the contrary,—should we have made public these negative or positively hostile conclusions? We could not have done so. We should simply have refrained from giving to the world any thoughts at all on the subject of the evidences of the Christian religion. These Thoughts, or any such thoughts, would never have seen the light of day. But if you had found the truth, it may be urged, even though it was against you, why should that truth be concealed and hushed up; why should it not be made known just as completely and just as honestly as though it were on your side?

Yes, if the truth had really been found; but we ask, with Pilate, "What is truth?"

Truth is not simply that which *is*, it is also that which is *worth having*. Would this discovery of ours as to the nothingness of religion from a scientific point of view be worth having? Whom would it benefit? The non-existence of God and of that world which we significantly call a better world, to whom would these grand negative discoveries of ours, these discoveries of darkness where we hoped there might possibly have been light, whom would they have been of any advantage to? Why, then, should they be allowed to go beyond the region of the discoverer's own thoughts? So far at least as he is concerned, whatever principles others may hold in the matter, had these Thoughts produced nothing worth having, or only what is of a questionable character, he would have proceeded no further from the moment he had been so unfortunate as to make that discovery.

We have, however, gone further, and not only have thought, but have said what we thought. The reader may safely be left to draw his own conclusions. And so, kind friend (and may we not add fellow-traveller), farewell!

www.ingramcontent.com/pod-product-compliance
Lightning Source LLC
Chambersburg PA
CBHW031250250426
43672CB00029BA/1735